BEAD DESIGN

a comprehensive course for beginner and experienced craftsman

by RUTH WASLEY and EDITH HARRIS

Crown Publishers, Inc., New York

To my husband, Bernard, and my daughter, Janet,
for tolerating my temporary abdication as wife and mother,
while the author emerged

RUTH WASLEY

To my husband, Seymour, and my children, who
have helped in ways too numerous to mention

EDITH HARRIS

BEAD DESIGN

Fabiana, Ranunculus,
and Mountain Laurel

Jewelry

Fruit

Oriental Blossom Tree

Contents

Acknowledgments

The Queens Botanical Society for their help and guidance

Hilly Wissot and Rudy Caggiano, who invited me to join their staff for the Continuing Education program at Junior High School 74

The New York City Board of Education for permitting me to be the "first" to teach Beaded Flowers within the city system

My good friends, the Cornell Group of Hollis Hills, for inspiring me

John Goeller for his excellent photography

Marlyn Dickenson for her unlimited help on "Arranging"

Norman Adler for his fine sketches

All my students for their encouragement and for acting as "guinea pigs"

RUTH WASLEY

Joan Wernick for her encouragement and advice

Jack Rosen for the fresh flowers needed to formulate some of the designs

EDITH HARRIS

Foreword

Many dedicated hours were spent by the authors to work out the details of the beautiful flowers included in this book.

Mrs. Wasley has spent a great deal of her time at the Queens Botanical Garden to acquaint herself with the structure and color scheme of the various flowers. In creating her designs she has successfully emulated nature.

The art of creating flowers with beads has become a hobby of widespread enjoyment. Mrs. Wasley has played an important part in the development of this craft with her excellent instruction.

It has been a pleasure to work with her.

MARTIN F. FLAYTER
Executive Director
Queens Botanical Garden Society, Inc.

1

Introduction

THE ART OF BEAD DESIGN was originally brought to the United States from France and had its vogue in the mid-Victorian era, when beads were used extensively on clothing and in home furnishings. All the women's weekly magazines of the day carried instructions for fancy beadwork, most popular of which were beaded flowers made from glass beads strung on fine wire. Then fashions changed, and little was heard of bead design for many years.

During the last few years, however, there has been a great resurgence of the art of creating with glass beads in the United States. Bead flowers are reaching new heights of popularity as home accessories, and designs other than flowers are constantly being introduced. Beautiful works are being made in the form of trees, fruit, animals, holiday ornaments, accessories, and even jewelry.

In this book we hope to introduce the subject of beading to the beginner, as well as to offer many new challenges to the more advanced craftsman. In writing it our aims were threefold: to set forth the content in a simple, compact, and orderly fashion; to present a book comprised *entirely* of original designs; and to show by photographs and drawings how to achieve the best results.

For convenience, we have arranged all the designs in alphabetical order under their popular or common names. The suggested colors in each of the designs are as close to nature as we could possibly make them. However, if you wish to vary any of these colors to suit your own taste, by all means do so.

We recommend that the beginner read the general instructions (Chapter 3) carefully, with wire and beads in hand. To start, select any of the flowers that are starred in the index, for they are the easiest to make. Try to use the materials listed for each particular design, as we had special reasons for selecting them. When more than one color is called for in a design, use the same type of bead throughout. Before beginning any work, read and understand all the instructions for that project. Pay special attention to details of assembling and shaping the design. They can make the difference between a lovely, realistic piece and a lifeless copy.

After you have mastered the techniques and completed the projects included in this book, it is our hope that you will continue to enjoy the craft of beading by creating original designs and new objects of your own.

THE GLASS BEAD

Because glass is older than written history, its origin can only be traced through archaeology. The first known glass bead was made by melting together silica, a major component of all sand, with certain other ingredients, such as soda and lime. (The soda hastens the melting of silica, and the lime hardens the finished product.)

The earliest known beads are believed to have been made about 12,000 B.C. They were found in Egypt but were most likely brought there from Asia. They were made of stone and covered with a green glaze. Their green color was the natural result of using crude sand and crude soda. The first hints of transparency appeared in translucent blue beads dated about 1570 B.C.

A molded glass bead was found at the site of Queen Ra-Ma-Ka's tomb, first Queen of the Egyptian Empire, who lived about 1447 B.C. Thousands of beads molded in the shape of flowers and fruits were produced around 1200 B.C., and small white cylinder beads were produced by the millions and used to decorate the wrappings of mummies.

Other lands throughout the Mediterranean area were producing beads by 1300 B.C. A new empire finally destroyed Egypt's importance in glass bead making. In 30 B.C. the Roman emperor added Egypt to his list of conquests and demanded tribute in glass. His demands kept the Egyptian foundries busy for forty years until the fires began to die about A.D. 14.

It was about this time that the Roman emperor ordered skilled glass workers from Egypt and Syria to migrate to Rome and establish a glass industry there. Glass making became a major industry, and beads became relatively unimportant among the many new products being produced.

In the thirteenth century a form of prayer using a string of beads was instituted by St. Dominic. The string, called a rosary, consisted at that time of 15 units of beads. Each unit contained 10 small beads, preceded by one larger one. A prayer was recited at every bead. Because of the length of the original rosary, it became customary to pay someone, usually a resident of an almshouse, to recite the prayers. These people were referred to as bede women (or men), and it was they who made the first bead flowers. Horsehair and human hair were used for stringing. The craft was handed down through the centuries and came to be associated with the Church and its decorations.

The American Indians, noted for their bead making, originally used porcupine quills for this art. Early traders from Europe were responsible for the introduction of colorful beads.

Beads, like anything else controlled by the whims of fashion, go through cycles of popularity. Around A.D. 1295 Venice made glass beads so beautifully that they became a fashion unto themselves. Tiny beads were sewn onto gowns. By Victorian days, Bohemia led in the world's glass bead production. When Bohemia became Czechoslovakia after World War I, that country became the largest source of supply. Shortly after the war ended, Czechoslovakia had over 700 glass bead exporters.

Today most of our beads come from France, Czechoslovakia, and Japan. They are available in an infinite variety of shapes, sizes, finishes, and colors.

2

Materials

BEADS

There is a wide variety of beads on the market, all of which are imported. Not all, however, are suitable for the art of bead design. For our purposes, only glass beads are used, and because loose beads are extremely unmanageable, we use only those already strung on thread. The following guide will help you with your selection.

Round "Seed" Beads

OPAQUE Usually referred to as "chalk," even though they are made of glass. No light shines through. They are considered informal.

LINED Clear crystal, lined with dye. The outer portion, of clear crystal, reflects some light, but the color within the bead is more prominent. These are generally used when very fragile colors are desired. Since they do glisten, they are more formal.

TRANSPARENT The color is in the glass itself, and the light shining through is what gives them their jewel-like appearance. This type of bead has the greatest variety of colors. They are considered formal.

Faceted Beads

CUT CRYSTAL These beads have facets cut into them and come round *or* long. We have used them occasionally, when they are best

suited for a particular design. Because they are rather elaborate, they should be used with reserve.

Stem Beads

Large beads that are used on stem wires. We have used them in green only, and the best size is 8/0 mm. Stem beads are used for finishing the stem of a flower or for the center veins of leaves.

SIZES

11/0 or 1.9 mm. are the easiest to use, since the wire fits through the holes of the beads very readily. The finished work is most attractive.

Beads are available in clusters of 10 or 12 strings. Some clusters contain strings with 18″ to 20″ of beads, while others contain strings with 40″ of beads. All of our designs were executed with the 40″ strings.

WIRE

The higher the number, the finer or thinner the wire. Gauge numbers, determined by the metal industry, are standard throughout the United States.

Beading Wire

Comes on a spool, like sewing thread. Sizes are marked by gauge, and the most often used are #26, #28, #32, and #34, in galvanized, annealed steel. In our designs we shall refer to them as *silver*. #26 and #28 are *working* wire. #32 is *binding*, or assembly, wire. #34 is *lacing* wire.

Brass gauges run a little differently. You will find the brass to be softer. We use gauges #25, #26, #28. In our designs they will be referred to as *gold*.

The color of the wire used is determined by the color of the beads. Some beads look better on gold, as it brings their color through stronger; for example, yellow crystal.

There are also enameled wires in various colors. They come in the same gauges as the galvanized. The green and red are used only where special effects are desired, as they tend to make the crystal beads look dull. However, some people have a great deal of acid in their systems, and as soon as they touch the galvanized wire, it turns black. In such cases we recommend using the enameled wire. We also recommend white enameled wire when working with white chalk beads.

Stem Wire

Used for mounting the flowers. It is usually available in 18″ lengths. The most frequently used sizes are gauge #14, 16, 18, and 20. There are two types: *galvanized* and *bright basic*. The galvanized is clean and bright, but it is too soft to hold up the heavier flowers securely. The bright basic is much firmer, and though it is not as attractive-looking as the galvanized, it will be covered with tape or beads anyway, so the appearance is of no consequence.

Floral Tape

Used in rolls ½″ wide. Each side is tacky when the tape is stretched. Many colors are available. Our designs will call for dark green, light green, brown, yellow, or white.

TOOLS

Wire cutter. An inexpensive one will do as well as the best. The most important thing is that it be sharp.

Long-nose pliers. Sometimes called needle-nose. It is best to have serrations on the inside, as they will grip the wire much more firmly than a smooth surface.

A small ruler.

A few thumbtacks.

A container to hold your equipment. We recommend an inexpensive fishing-tackle box, as it has compartments in which to keep your beads and a section below in which to keep your tools and wires. This can be carried around very easily.

You may also like to work over a thin piece of soft plastic foam or a piece of felt so that you can easily retrieve any beads you may drop.

MATERIALS NEEDED FOR PLANTING

Clay

The weight of the flowers makes it necessary to use clay. Styrofoam will not hold them upright. The best kind of clay to use is plasteline, as it is nonhardening. Instructions for using the clay will be explained more fully in the chapter on flower arranging.

Sheet Moss

This is "live" moss and is used to cover the clay. Do not purchase the dyed moss, as it looks too artificial and detracts from your arrangement. Air Fern may also be used to cover the clay.

Fish Chips

In some designs, where plaster of Paris is used for planting, we cover the plaster with fish chips, which can be purchased in a pet shop or garden supply store. We use only green or black, and the glass chips look best.

If you are unable to locate a source for materials, you may write to the author in care of the publisher.

3

General

Instructions

1. Starting

a. Insert a thumbtack into the top of your spool of wire.

b. Open the spool and unwind a few feet of wire.

c. Anchor the wire around the thumbtack so that the rest of the spool does not unwind. Always work with the wire *attached* to the spool until a petal is completed. It is advisable to clean the wire before stringing the beads. Run a paper napkin across the opened wire a few times.

d. Cut the open end of the wire at an angle to obtain a sharp point.

e. Remove one string of beads from a cluster. Knot one end of the string. On the opposite end, gently insert the wire into the beads.

f. Transfer the beads from the string to the wire by withdrawing the string after you pick up the beads. Put one or two strings on the wire at one time. After all the beads have been transferred, make a tiny loop on the end of the wire, so the beads won't slide off.

2. Basic Procedure

a. Start with 3″ of *bare* wire at the knotted end of the spool.

b. Just *under* the 3″, slide up the "basic" amount of beads called for in the design. Hold these beads between the thumb and index finger of one hand.

c. Make a loop of bare wire, about 6″ long, between the beads and the spool. Twist the loop several times to secure.

d. Release the beads you have been holding and let them slip down against the twist in the lower loop. They should float freely on the upper single wire.

These beads are the "basic" count, around which the design is formed.

The upper single wire is the "top basic" wire.

The lower loop is the "bottom basic" loop (sometimes referred to as the stem of the petal).

The wire still connected to the spool is the "feed" wire.

NOTE: Make sure your top and bottom basic wires are always in a straight vertical line.

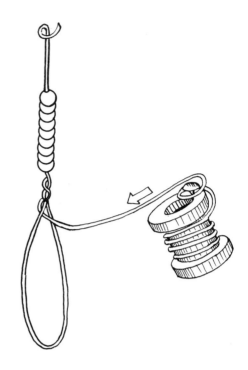

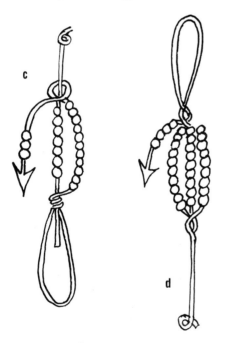

REMEMBER: Cross each basic wire in a full circle before starting the next row.

REMEMBER: Rotate your petal with only *one* side facing front at all times.

g. each line of beads counts as one row. The original basic count is also considered one row.

3. Round Petals

Start as in Basic Procedure.

a. Bring the feed wire up, next to the basic count, with enough beads to fit parallel to the top of the basic count. Always work to the right of the basic (unless you are left-handed, in which case, of course, work to the left side).

b. Hold both rows of beads firmly, near the top.

c. With bare feed wire, cross in *front* of the top basic wire. Bring your feed wire around the *back* and then cross in *front* again. This will form a complete circle around the top basic wire. Make sure you form a true right angle, as this will keep your petal round.

d. Rotate the petal in a clockwise motion. Only *one* side should face you at all times. (This creates a front and a back to the petal.) The bottom basic loop is now facing *up* and the top basic wire is facing *down*.

e. Repeat steps a, b, and c. This time at step c you will be crossing the bottom basic loop. You will still make a complete circle by crossing in front, going around the back, and crossing in front again.

f. Continue around the petal in the same manner for the number of rows given in the design.

h. When the petal is completed, twist all wires firmly, two or three times, *directly* under the beads. Do not twist down stem.

i. Cut feed wire away from bottom basic loop at this point. Be sure to knot the feed wire immediately, so your beads will not slide off.

j. Bend the top basic wire to the back of the petal and cut away all but ⅛″. Press this firmly against the petal.

NOTE: If you run out of beads before completing a petal, estimate how much wire you will need for finishing by measuring around the petal with bare wire for the unfinished number of rows. Add an inch or two to be safe. Cut wire away from the spool at this point and string additional beads on the open end. Do not forget to knot the wire at the open end so that the beads will not slide off.

REFINEMENT: Keep each row as close to the previous one as possible. Be sure you have ample beads on the wire each time you make a new row. Too few will permit bare wire to show. Too many will make the petal too loose.

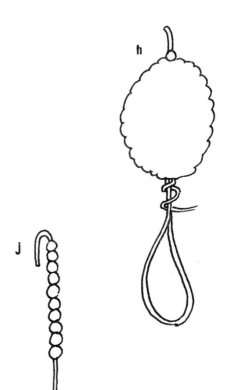

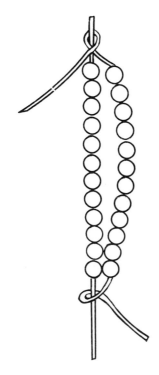

4. Pointed Petals

The procedure is the same as for a round petal, until the second row.

a. When the second row is parallel to the basic count, add *2 extra beads* before crossing your basic wire.

b. Cross the top basic wire at an angle. This will bring your feed wire to a higher point than the previous row.

c. Complete the circle around the top basic wire.

d. Flatten the angle *against* the top basic wire.

e. Rotate the petal. Push the third row of beads firmly into the space created by the angle.

f. Finish the third row as called for in the design. (Some designs have petals pointed at one end, some at both ends.) Start a pointed top at the end of the second row, a pointed bottom at the end of the third row.

g. Continue around the petal for the required number of rows and end in the same manner as a round petal.

NOTE: In order to maintain the pointed effect, the extra beads must be added every time you reach the pointed end of the petal.

NOTE: For a "semipointed" petal, add only 1 extra bead at the point.

ELONGATING: When elongating is called for, work in the same manner as a pointed petal, except for the angle at the basic wire. Create a *sharper* angle.

5. Domed Petals

a. Start with a normal round petal.

b. After row 4 is completed, draw both top and bottom basic wires down into a vertical position, with front of petal facing up. (It should look like a table with two legs.)

c. Continue working around each basic wire, working one row *under* another. Make sure you keep both hanging wires completely vertical. If they swing out to the sides, your petal will get too wide.

d. Domed petals have an even number of rows; therefore, you will end at the top basic wire.

e. Twist feed wire around top basic wire and cut away an even length to match the top basic wire.

NOTE: Do not forget to make a complete circle each time you reach the top and bottom basic wires.

6. Loop Petals

a. Knot the end of the wire.

b. Leave 3″ of bare wire, then measure the required number of beads called for in the design.

c. Form these beads into a loop.

d. Twist the wires twice, *just under the beads,* to hold firmly.

e. To make several loops all on 1 continuous wire, make each loop next to another, about 1/16″ apart. Be sure to twist *each* loop twice at the base before making the next one. Always work across the wire in *one* direction only so that you do not incorporate the beginning wire with successive loops.

f. Continue until the required number of loops is completed.

g. Leave 3″ of free wire after the last loop and cut away from spool.

NOTE: If a design calls for a 2″ loop, measure the 2″ of beads *before* forming into a loop.

7. Wrap Petals

a. Leave 3″ of bare wire.

b. Form a loop with number of beads given in the design.

c. Twist wires twice *directly* under the beads.

d. With beads, wrap around the outside of the first loop. Keep the second row as close to the first as possible.

e. Twist twice, directly below the beads, around the original wire.

f. Continue for the required number of "wraps." The first loop is not included as a wrap. Example: Wrap twice would make 3 rows in all.

g. Continuous wraps are done in the same way as continuous loops. However, more wire must be left between each set of wraps to accommodate the beads.

8A. Crossover Petals (4-row)

a. Leave 3″ of bare wire.

b. Make a loop of the required size, press it closed, twist twice *directly* below the beads.

c. Bring the beaded wire up inside the first loop to the top of the oval. This will make the third row.

d. Press *bare* wire down into the space between the top 2 beads and bring the feed wire down the back of the petal.

e Turn over and fully fill this space with beads to meet the twist of the first loop made.

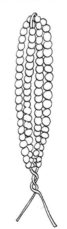

f. Twist the spool wire around the stem twice and cut it free at about 3″.

NOTE: If the design calls for multiple petals, *do not cut wire free* from spool, but continue on the same wire for the specified number of petals.

8B. Crossover Petals (3-row)

Follow steps a, b, and c of 4-row crossover.

d. Bring only bare wire down the back.

e. Continue as in a 4-row crossover.

9. Horizontal Petals

a. Make a long top basic with *bare* wire only (no beads). Make a long bottom basic loop.

b. Form a horizontal loop of beads on *one side* of the top basic wire. (Aim the loop from the bottom basic toward the top basic.)

c. Narrow the loop.

d. Go around the top basic wire for one complete turn.

e. Repeat the same size loop on the opposite side of the top basic wire. (This time aim the loop from the top basic toward the bottom basic wire.)

f. Go around the bottom basic loop for one complete turn.

g. The successive rows should be close to one another. There is no need to measure the beads.

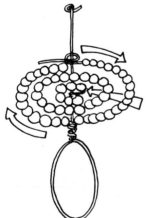

h. Continue working around, encircling the top and bottom basic wires, until the required number of rows is completed. Count from the outside *across* the petal to determine the number of rows.

NOTE: For a neat petal, keep the rows close to one another as you work back and forth.

10. Split Basic Petals

a. Start like a normal petal, but leave a long bottom basic loop.

b. Work one petal as instructed in the design. *Do not* cut away from spool.

c. Unwind the lower basic loop until only 2 twists remain under the petal.

d. Cut the basic loop in half at the bottom.

e. Twist the feed wire around *one* leg of this split, enough times to equal the space on the first petal, between the bottom of the basic count and the bottom of the petal.

f. This leg becomes the next top basic wire.

g. Slide the basic count of beads on to this new top basic wire.

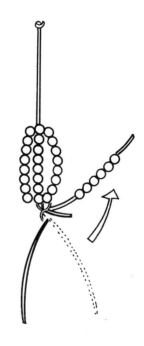

h. Continue with the beads on the spool to complete a second petal. This will give you a two-petal unit on 1 wire.

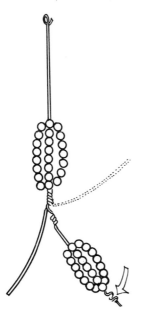

i. Finish in the usual manner, joining the second leg and the feed wire as a stem.

NOTE: To make a three-petal unit on 1 wire, use the method just described, but utilize *both* legs of the split. The feed wire alone becomes the stem of the petal.

11. Lacing

Lacing is a process of adding firmness to a petal or of joining petals together by "back-stitching."

Joining Petals Together

a. Cut a piece of lacing wire (#34) 3 times the width of the area to be laced.
b. Hold the petal with front side facing you and the top basic wire facing up.
c. Start on the right side of the petal.
d. Push 2″ of lacing wire to the wrong side of the petal. The long end remains in front.
e. Holding both pieces of wire, draw them out to the right until wire is caught between 2 beads.

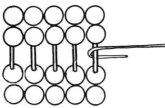

f. Anchor the lacing wire by drawing the long end only around the outside of the petal and then through to the front again between the first and second rows.

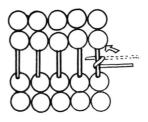

g. Use the following procedure to "back-stitch":

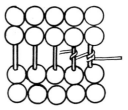

Using only the long end of the lacing wire from now on, draw it around the outside of the petal again, across the back to Row 2.

Push the lacing wire to the front on the *left* side of Row 2.

Pull the wire across Row 2 and go to the back on the *right* side of Row 2.

Push the wire to the front on the *left* side of Row 3.

Pull the wire across Row 3 and go to the back on the *right* side of Row 3.

Continue in this manner until all rows are laced together.

When joining the next petal, treat it as a continuation of the first one.

When all petals are joined together, end the lacing by going around the last row twice.

Leave 2″ and cut away the rest.

Further instructions will be given in the individual design.

Adding Firmness to a Petal

The procedure is the same as joining petals together, but you start and finish in a different manner.

a. Cut your lacing wire 3 times the width of the petal to be laced.

b. Fold it in half.

c. With front of petal facing you, straddle the center basic row halfway down the petal and catch the fold of the wire between 2 beads.

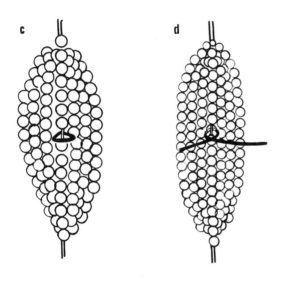

d. Crisscross the wire in the back of the petal and lace across half the petal with one half of the lacing wire.

e. Turn the petal upside down with front side still facing you and lace across the other half. Lace with same backstitch as procedure for joining petals.

f. When every row is laced, "overcast" each end by bringing the lacing wire *under* the little bar created by the backstitch. Pull up on wire and go *over* the bar to the back.

g. Cut lacing wire off close to petal.

12. Assembly

Instructions for assembling the various items will be given with each design. However, there are some generalities to know beforehand.

Floral Tape

There is no right or wrong side to the tape. It is not tacky until it is stretched.

a. Tear or cut a length away from the roll.

b. Stretch it to make it tacky.

c. Starting at one end of the stem, fold the tape over the tip of the wire and press it firmly against the stem.

d. Tape diagonally down the entire stem, pressing the tape against the stem wire as you work. The sharper you angle the tape, the slimmer your stem will be.

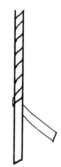

NOTE: If you run out of tape before you finish the entire stem, just add another piece at that point and continue.

Hooking on the Stem Wire

a. Hold the tip of the stem wire in the tip of the pliers.

b. Give the pliers one-half turn. This will create a ½″ to ¾″ hook. Assembly instructions will tell at what point to insert the hook and how to continue.

Binding Petals or Leaves to the Stem

a. Hold #32 binding wire very securely against the stem.

b. Bring the bottom of the petal or leaf close to the stem wire, with the hanging stems downward.

c. Wind the wire very tightly around the stem, catching in the hanging wires of the petal.

d. Each leaf or petal is attached one at a time with the same piece of binding wire. (Detailed instructions will be given in the design.)

e. When all petals have been joined to the stem, go around the stem with the binding wire another two turns and cut away.

NOTE: If you find you are not binding tightly enough, try wearing a leather glove for a better grip.

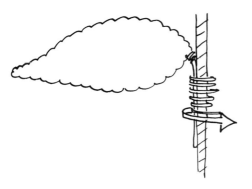

Tapering and Shortening Stems

a. Gently pull the hanging wires slightly away from the stem.

b. Cut the wires at different levels and trim some out almost to the binding wire.

c. Be sure all loops have been cut away from the hanging wires.

d. Explicit lengths, or further instruction, will be given with each design.

HOW TO INTERPRET A TYPICAL DESIGN FORMULA

Materials will be listed first. Only *crystal* beads are used for foliage; therefore, only color suggestion will be noted, not type of bead.

The wrong side of petals or leaves will be referred to as the "back." The right side will be referred to as the "front."

Petals:	Basic 5	Round top	[6]
#26 silver	Rows 11	Pointed bottom	
Centers:	Six 8-bead loops, all on one		[1]
#28 silver	wire		
	Keep all loops round.		
Leaves:	Basic 1″	Pointed top	[3]
#26 green	Rows 9	and bottom	

Petals = part of individual flower.

#26 silver = gauge of working wire.

Basic 5 = 5 *beads* for basic count.

Rows 11 = number of rows when counting across *entire* petal.

Round top, pointed bottom } = shaping of petal as you work.

[6] = number of petals for *one individual* flower. (If several flowers are needed for a branch, this will be indicated in the design.)

Leaves = same as petals, only this time the basic count is given in *inches*.

Sometimes a specific method of working is required, in which case the part will be starred and the method named. Example:

Leaves:	Basic 1″	Work even for 9 rows,
	Rows 32*	then:
		* Use V split, and continue for the remainder of rows.

or

Petals: *Horizontal Petal
Basic 8
Rows 8   etc.

4

Advanced Procedures

These generalities are helpful to know before you begin to follow the more specific information that accompanies each design.

1. Reverse Basic
2. Bracing a Leaf
3. Using Stem Beads as a Basic
4. Lantern Assembly
5. Jeweling the Stem
6. Single Beaded Units
7. Branch Petals or Leaves
8. V Split
9. Weaving
10. Refinements

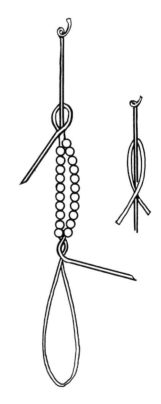

1. Reverse Basic

This procedure is used where petals are curled back sharply and you wish to conceal the wires on the visible parts.

Beading is done in the usual manner with the following exception: When crossing the top basic wire, bring the feed wire around the back first, then cross in front, and go around the back again.

As the name suggests, it is just a reverse of the usual basic crossing.

The bottom basic is crossed in the normal way.

2. Bracing a Leaf

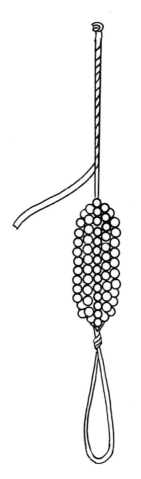

Method I

a. Leave a long top basic wire on the leaf. Finish the entire leaf, but *do not* cut away the top basic wire.

b. Shorten the bottom basic wires to 2″.

c. Tape a piece of #18 stem wire, equal to the length of the leaf plus the hanging stem.

d. With the tip of the stem wire touching the tip of the leaf, wind the top basic wire of the leaf around one end of the stem wire.

e. Tape the exposed wire.

f. Draw the stem down the back of the leaf and tape the stem wire to the hanging wires of the leaf.

g. Secure the stem wire to the leaf with a small piece of lacing wire through the center of the leaf. Twist the lacing wire a few times and cut it short.

Method II

a. Tape a piece of #18 stem wire.

b. Secure the beaded spool wire around it, 6″ up from the bottom.

c. Tape the exposed wire.

d. Rest the basic count against the stem wire and use the *stem wire* as the top and bottom basic wire.

e. Cross the stem wire in the same manner as you would your normal basic wires.

3. Using Stem Beads As a Basic ▶

When a leaf is particularly large, or for a special effect, stem beads are used for the basic count.

a. Tape a #20 stem wire for the correct number of inches called for in the design.

b. Push stem beads on to the stem wire.

c. Tape above the stem beads.

d. Secure the open end of the beaded spool wire under the stem beads.

e. Tape the exposed spool wire.

f. Proceed in the usual manner, counting the stem beads as the basic row.

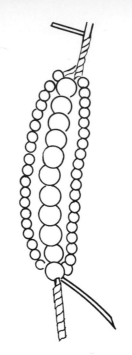

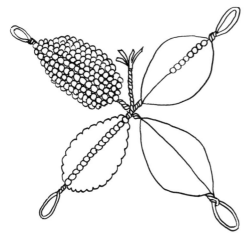

◀ 4. Lantern Assembly

a. Complete the number of petals specified in the design.

b. *Do not* cut away top basic wires.

c. Shape each petal.

d. With the back of each petal facing up, have all tips touching.

e. Twist all the top basic wires together.

f. Cut away all but ¾″ of this wire.

g. With the back of the petals facing *each other* and the ¾″ of wire enclosed, bring all petals together at the base.

h. Twist the bottom basic wires together.

5. Jeweling the Stem ▶

This is done in the same shade of green used for the foliage of the flower.

a. String green on #32 wire. (Approximately 5″ is equal to 1″ of jeweling.)

b. With the free end of the wire, start from 1″ under the flower head, and spiral the bare wire upward with 3 or 4 turns until just under the flower head.

c. Tape the exposed wire.

d. Push the beads toward the stem.

e. Wind down the stem with the beads, keeping the rows close together. Do not permit bare wire to show.

f. When jeweling is the required length, wind the bare wire around the stem 3 times and cut away from the spool.

g. Cover the bare wire with a small piece of tape.

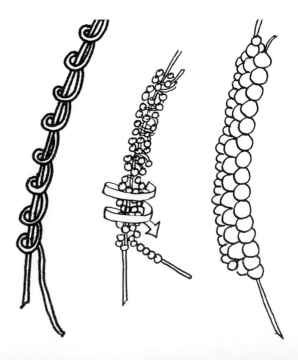

There are various ways of finishing the stems of flowers, depending upon the effect desired. Explicit instructions for other methods will be given in each design.

6. Single Beaded Units ▶

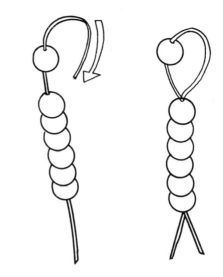

Method I

a. String beads on #34 lacing wire.
b. Leave a long piece of bare wire at the beginning of the spool.
c. Insert the open end of the wire back through the beads, omitting the *first* bead.
d. Push the wire through the required number of beads.
e. Pull the wire tightly until the first bead is resting on top of the rest of the beads.
f. Twist the wire at the base and cut it away from the spool.

Method II

a. String beads on the gauge wire called for in the design.
b. Coil the open end of the wire around a needle 5 times.

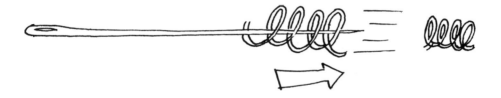

c. Squeeze the coil closely together with the tips of the pliers and remove the needle.
d. Cut the coil so that 2 full circles remain.
e. Push the required number of beads close to the coil.
f. Make a basic loop under the beads so that the beads are pushed firmly against the coil.
g. Measure the required number of beads.

h. Pressing the needle tightly against these last beads, again coil the wire around a needle 5 times.
i. Squeeze the coil closed and remove the needle.
j. Cut the coil through the center.
You are now ready to continue, if necessary, with the first coil of the next unit already made.

7. Branch Petals or Leaves

These are leaves or petals with loops added to each side.

a. Start as usual and work the required number of rows.

b. Measure the size of the loop as instructed in the design.

c. Fold the wire with enough beads to form an *outcurving* loop.

d. Cross in front of the bottom hanging wire, go around to the back, and bring the feed wire through to the front again *between* the *original petal* and the *new loop*.

e. Repeat the loop on the opposite side, but this time make a complete turn around the bottom hanging wire.

f. Repeat this process for the necessary number of loops.

g. End the petal in the usual manner.

NOTE: The feed wire is brought from the back to the front between the 2 outside loops on *one* side only. The opposite side is done completely around the bottom hanging wire.

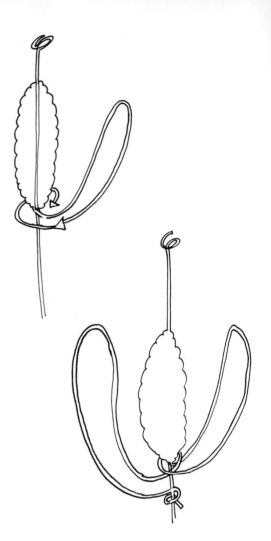

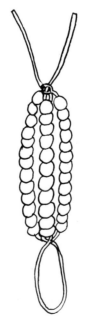

8. V Split

a. Make a *loop* as a top basic instead of a single wire. Twist the loop several times and cross it as you would a single top basic.

b. Work for the specified number of rows.

c. Untwist the loop until 1 twist remains under the beads.

d. Split the top basic in half, through the center, creating a V.

e. With the bare wire, make a complete circle around one leg of the V and work back on the same side.

f. Cross the basic in the usual way and work to the other leg of the V. Continue in this manner for the number of rows given in the design.

The V split can also be used on the bottom basic wire. The method of working is the same.

More explicit information will accompany the design when this procedure is necessary.

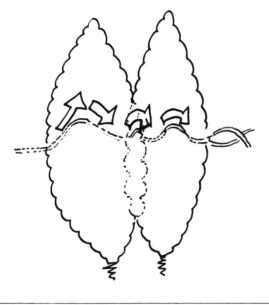

9. Weaving

This is used when it is necessary to keep a flower in a particular shape.

a. cut a piece of #34 lacing wire about 12" long.

b. Secure firmly at one end of petal.

c. Weave in and out among the rows of each petal until you reach the starting point.

d. Pull the wire as tightly as you desire the flower to close.

e. Join both ends of lacing wire and twist for ¾".

f. Cut away all but the ¾" and tuck this into the inside of the flower.

10. Refinements

The following hints are meant to make your work easier and neater.

a. Hair clips make handy supports when working very large leaves or petals. Clip one across the beads about ⅓ up from the bottom or ⅓ down from the top. When you are ready to add a new row, work up to the hair clip, open it, slip the beads under, close it, and continue working.

b. If too much wire shows when working on red, cover the wire with red nail polish. When working on black, use black dry marker to cover any overly conspicuous wire.

c. Should beads spill while working, the best way to pick them up is by rolling a lint remover across the area. This is especially helpful on carpeting.

d. To make loops rounder, insert an orangewood stick or a slim pencil through the loop. To make loops oval, insert the tip of the needle-nose pliers.

e. Hanging stems should be smooth before taping. Never twist *down* the wire, as this makes them very bulky. Twist *directly* below the beads, cut the feed wire away very close to the stem, and let the remaining wires hang down straight.

f. When beading hanging stems of leaves or petals, always keep the final twisting as close under the beads as possible. Cut the feed wire very *close* to the stem.

5

Flowers

Flowers are so widely enjoyed, and there is such a large selection to choose from, that we have made them the primary object of the book.

Pick and choose to your heart's content, and you will no doubt make them *all* in due time. If you scan the chapter on flower arranging before starting, it will help you select the flowers that are most harmonious for a centerpiece. Perhaps you would prefer to start with your favorites and take it from there.

ANDROMEDA

Materials

#28 gold wire for flowers
#26 silver wire for leaves
White alabaster for flowers
Medium green for leaves
Pale green tape
#18 stem wire

Start each unit with 6″ of bare wire. Make all loops round.

Flower 1: 10 12 bead loops with 2 beads between loops, all on one wire   [1]
Flower 2: 15—15-bead loops as above   [2]
Flower 3: 20—15-bead loops as above   [2]

Complete each unit in the following manner: Start with the first loop made and spiral the entire unit around the 6″ of bare wire. Join both units of Flower 2 by twisting the hanging wires together. Treat as one flower. Do the same for Flower 3.

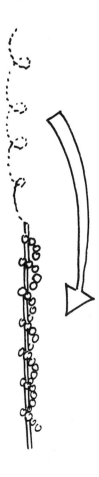

Leaves:	Basic ¾″ Rows 3	Pointed top and bottom	[5]
	Basic ¾″ Rows 5	As above	[3]
	Basic 1″ Rows 7	As above	[5]

Tape hanging wires of each leaf.

Assembly:

a. Tape a 10″ piece of #18 stem wire.
b. Tape the first flower to the top of the stem.
c. Tape the second flower directly under the first.
d. Tape the third flower directly under the second.
e. Tape the first 5 leaves to the stem next to each other (in a semicircle) just under and behind the flower.
f. The next 3 leaves are taped on ½″ under in a triangle.
g. The last 5 leaves are taped on ½″ under to fit all around stem.
h. Tape down remainder of stem.

Shaping:

First 5 leaves nestle around stem, tips curled downward.
The rest of the leaves are pushed close to the stem with the tips curled sharply downward.
The flowers droop down over the leaves.

ANTHURIUM

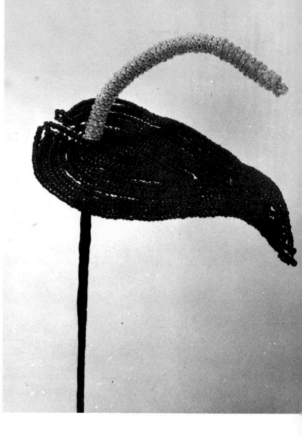

Materials

#26 silver wire for petal
#32 binding wire
#34 lacing wire
Bright red or alabaster white crystal for petal
White and yellow crystal for stamen
White and dark green tape
#16 stem wire

String 3 double strands of petal color on #26 wire.
Start with a 6″ loop for the top basic, and a 15″ loop for the bottom basic. Lace across the petal as you work.

Petal: V split method
     Basic 5   Round top
     Rows 33*   Pointed bottom

*After completing the fifth row, cut the top basic loop in half. Proceed as in a V split. Keep the legs of the split close together.
When 33 rows are completed, end the petal at the bottom basic. Cut away the feed wire and continue as follows:
a. String enough beads on each leg of the split to cover the edge.

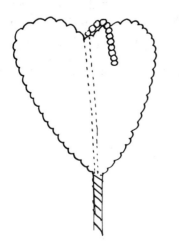

b. Bring the open point of each leg down to the narrow part of the V on the front of the petal.
c. Draw both wires through to the back of the petal and twist them together.
d. Bring the bottom basic down along the back of the petal and twist all wires together.
e. Tape all hanging wires in green.

Stamen: String 1 double strand of white on the #32 wire, then add 5″ of yellow. Tape a #16 stem wire with white tape. Starting at the top, jewel the stem for 4″ with the colors on the #32 wire.

Assembly:
a. Set the stamen into the point of the V on the petal with the jeweling standing up.
b. Tape the hanging wires of the petal to the stamen stem with green tape.
c. Bend the stamen top, to arc over the petal, toward the point.
d. Bend the point of the petal sharply downward.

APPLE BLOSSOM
BRANCH

Materials

#25 gold wire
Pink and white crystal for flower
Medium and dark green for foliage
Brown tape
#16 stem wire

Each branch has 5 flowers and 10 leaves.

Centers: Medium green
6—6-bead loops, all on one wire [1]

Petals: String as follows for each individual petal: 9 white, 15 pink, 10 white, 11 pink, 7 white, 4 pink.
Basic 7   Round top   [5]
Rows 5   Pointed bottom

Leaves: Medium green on wire, add dark*
Basic 7   Pointed top
Rows 9*   Round bottom
* After completing 7 rows, estimate enough wire for 2 more rows. Cut free from spool and string on dark green to complete leaf.

Assembly:

a. Place 3 petals on top of one another, front sides up. Place 2 petals on top of these, front sides down. Twist all hanging wires together.
b. Fan out petals to form a circle.
c. Slide in the center and twist hanging wires once more.
d. Tape hanging stems.
e. Tape a #16 stem wire.
f. Tape 1 flower with 1″ of stem showing to the top of the stem wire.
g. Tape 2 leaves just under the flower, opposite each other.
h. Continue to tape down stem, adding 1 flower and 2 leaves, 1″ apart.

Shaping:

All flowers face front. Leaves are bent upward.

ASTER, BLUE JACKET

Materials

#26 and #28 silver wire
Yellow crystal for the centers
Blue or purple crystal for the flower and buds
Light green for foliage
Light green tape
#16 and #18 stem wire

Each branch has 3 flowers, 11 leaves, and 2 buds.

Center 1: #28	5—10-bead loops, all on one wire	[1]
Center 2: #28	6—15-bead loops, all on one wire	[1]
Petals: #26	15—2″ loops, all on one wire	[1]
Bud: #26	12—2″ loops, all on one wire	[1]
Flower Calyx: #28	8—1″ loops, all on one wire	[1]
Bud Calyx: #28	5—1″ loops, all on one wire	[1]

Leaves: #26	Basic 10 Rows 7	Pointed top Round bottom	[5]
	Basic 12 Rows 9	As above	[6]

Assembly of Flower:

a. Tape the hanging wires of all leaves.
b. Form Center 1 into a cluster.
c. Set Center 2 around cluster. Twist all hanging wires directly under the beads.
d. Close the petal into a circle. Insert center unit and twist hanging wires again. Tape hanging wires.
e. Tape a 6″ piece of #18 stem wire and tape flower to the top.
f. Tape calyx to stem just under the flower.
g. Tape 2 large leaves 1½″ under the flower, opposite one another; ½″ of leaf stem shows.

Assembly of Bud:

a. Cluster all loops to sit straight up.

b. Tape to the top of a 6″ piece of #18 stem wire.
c. Tape bud calyx in place and set the loops evenly around bud.
d. Tape down and add 1 small leaf 1″ below with ½″ of stem showing.

Assembly of Branch:

a. Tape a full length of #16 stem wire.
b. Tape a small leaf to the top with ½″ of leaf stem showing.
c. Add a bud stem 1″ below, with 2″ of stem showing, on one side of the main stem.
d. Tape 2″ of the flower stem 1″ below on the opposite side.
e. Place a small leaf just under flower.
f. Add another small leaf just under, and a second flower stem on the opposite side.
g. Add a bud stem and a final flower stem, each 1″ down, and opposite one another.

ASTER, CHINA

Materials

#25 gold wire for flowers and foliage
#32 binding wire
Pink or purple crystal
Medium green for foliage
Light green tape
#16 stem wire

Each flower unit is made all on one wire.

Center:	6—1″ loops	[1]
Row 1:	5—2″ loops	[3]
Row 2:	5—2½″ loops	[3]
Row 3:	5—3″ loops	[4]
Row 4:	5—3¼″ loops	[4]
Row 5:	5—2¾″ loops	[4]
Leaves:	3—2″ loops, all on one wire	[3]
	An individual 3″ loop	[3]
Calyx:	4—1½″ loops plus a 2½″ loop, all on one wire	[3]

Assembly:

a. Close all loops gently together.
b. Tape one end of a stem wire for 3″.
c. Bind the center to the top and tape the bindings.
d. Bind on each row evenly around stem. Tape binding.
e. Join the calyx into a circle by twisting the hanging wires together.

f. Set stem through circle with bare wires hanging down.
g. Press firmly up into flower and bind on.
h. Taper and cut all hanging wires, then tape down stem.
i. Spiral each leaf loop into a figure eight. Tape the single ones 1″ under the flower and 1″ under each other, evenly around stem.
j. Add the triple units in the same manner.

Shaping:

Outer petals stand straight out with the tips bent down.
The fourth row will follow this curve. All other petals are curled every which way, to look "shaggy."
The short petals of the calyx are pushed up against flower. The long ones are bent down.
The leaves stand straight up, with the tips bent back.

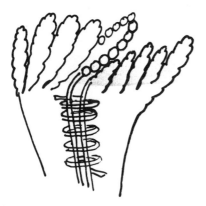

ASTER, WILD

Materials

#28 silver or #25 gold wire for flower and foliage
#32 binding wire
Any color crystal for flower plus a contrast for the centers
Medium green for foliage
Dark green tape
#16 stem wire

Petals: 9—1¾″ loops—3-row crossovers, all on one wire

Centers: 1¼″ open loop—3-row cross-over   [1]

Calyx: 4—1″ loops with a ¾″ loop underneath each one, all on one wire [1]

Leaves: Fern type*
11—1¼″ loops with seven beads between loops   [3]
7—1¼″ loops with seven beads between loops

* Procedure: Make 2 loops on each side of the wire with 7 beads between each pair. Work up to the top and make a single loop. With beads, work back down the stem to form a double beaded stem.

Assembly:

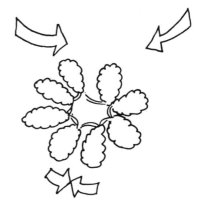

a. Cross the ending wire back to the starting point and work back and forth between loops of petals until wire is *halfway* around circle.
b. Slide center across petals so that all hanging wires are parallel.
c. Twist all hanging wires behind petals and hook on a #16 stem wire.
d. Close hook.
e. Thin out and shorten hanging wires to ¾″.
f. Tape the exposed ¾″ of wires to the stem wire.
g. Jewel down the stem with green on #32, for ¾″.
h. End jeweling and tape remainder of stem.
i. Tape on the 7-loop leaves 3″ below the flower head.
j. Tape on the next 3 leaves ½″ below the first 3.

ASTILBE

Materials
#25 gold wire
Multishaded pink and raspberry crystal for flower
Light green for foliage
Light green tape
#16 and #18 stem wire

Floret: Multishaded pink
   UNIT 1:   3–1″ loops all on one wire   [11]
                Close and spiral each loop.
   UNIT 2:   3–1½″ loops as above   [9]

Floret: Raspberry
   UNIT 3:   3–1½″ loops as above   [3]
   UNIT 4:   4–1¾″ loops as above   [3]
   UNIT 5:   4–2″ loops as above   [3]

Multishaded pink, branch method: Start with 4″ of bare wire. Make a 2″ beaded loop, then add 3–2″ loops on each side. Close and spiral each loop.   [6]

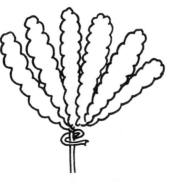

Leaves: Basic 10   Pointed top   [6]
              Rows 9   and bottom

Assembly of Leaf Branch:
a. Tape the hanging wires of all leaves.
b. Tape 2–6″ pieces of #18 stem wire.
c. Tape 3 leaves to the top of each piece of stem wire.

Assembly:
a. Tape a #16 stem wire.
b. Tape 2 of Unit 1 to the top.
c. Add 3 more of Unit 1, ¼″ under and evenly spaced around. Continue to add 3 more of this size in the same manner.
d. Continue adding 3 units of each succeeding size in the same manner, ¼″ under one another.
e. Add a leaf branch on each side 2″ under the flower with 4″ of stem showing.

Shaping:
All florets angle up and out.
Bend the leaf branch up with the top bent
    back.

27

AUTUMN LEAVES

Materials
#25 gold wire for leaves
#30 gold lacing wire
Yellow, orange, and pale green crystal
Brown tape

String a few inches of each color on to wire, using more yellow and orange, until there are 36″ of beads on the spool. Then add 1½″ of orange, 1″ of pale green, 1″ of orange, and 8″ of yellow.

Unit 1:	Basic 2″	Pointed top	[1]
	Rows 13	and bottom	
Unit 2:	Basic 1¾″	Pointed top	
	Rows 9	and bottom	

Make [1] all orange.
Make [1] all yellow.

Lace the three units together as illustrated. Tape the hanging wires. These look attractive when joined into groups of 3 or 4 units.

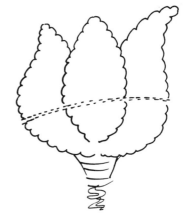

BEGONIA

Materials
#26 silver or #25 gold wire for flower
#26 silver wire for foliage
#32 binding wire
Yellow, red, salmon, or pink crystal for flower
Dark green for foliage
Dark green tape
#16 stem wire

Center:	Split basic	Basic 3 Rows 7	Round top Pointed bottom	[1]
Row 1:	Split basic	Basic 3 Rows 9	Round top Pointed bottom	[3]
Row 2:	Split basic	Basic 5 Rows 9	Round top Pointed bottom	[3]
Row 3:	Horizontal petal	Basic 10 Rows 12	Round top Pointed bottom	[5]
Leaves:	V split;	(use a 6″ loop for bottom basic). Basic 7 Rows 16*	Pointed top Round bottom	[2]

a. *After completing Row 8, create a V split on the bottom basic loop.

b. Proceed as in a V split until 16 rows are completed.
c. End leaf at the top basic wire.
d. Cut away feed wire.
e. String 6 beads on each leg of the V.

f. Bring the open point of each leg down to the narrow part of the V on the front of the petal.
g. Draw both wires through to the back of the petal and twist them together.
h. Bring the top basic down along the back of the petal and twist all wires together.
i. Cut away all but 1 wire and string 2″ of green on this wire.

j. Tape directly below the 2″ of green.

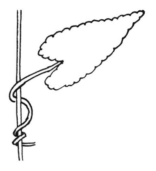

Assembly:

a. Set the center petals straight up and curl one over the other.
b. Twist the hanging stems just under the petals.
c. Hook a #16 stem wire through center.
d. Close the hook and tape hanging wires to stem wire for 1″.
e. Bind on petals of Row 1, one at a time, with #32 wire.
f. Space evenly around and just under center unit.
g. Bind on the next rows in the same manner just under one another.
h. Thin out all hanging wires and tape to stem.
i. Tape down remainder of stem.
j. Tape the leaves 2½″ under the flower, one on each side of the stem. *Two inches of leaf stem extends away from the main branch.

Shaping:

Petals sit straight out with the tips curled downward.
*Leaf also looks attractive if you curl the two inches around the main stem.

BLACK-EYED SUSAN

Materials

#25 gold and #26 silver wire
Black for centers
Yellow chalk or crystal for petals
Dark green and a few strands of light green
for foliage
Dark green tape
#16 stem wire

Centers:	Basic 5	Dome petal	[1]
#26	Rows 10		
Petals:	6—2″ 3-row crossovers, all on one		
#25	wire		[2]
Leaves:	Dark green on the wire, add 3¼″		
#26	of light green for each leaf.		
	Basic 1″	Pointed top	[3]
	Rows 11	Round bottom	

Assembly:

a. Set the 2 petal units on top of one another
and twist hanging wires.
b. Open and fan out the petals in a circle.
c. Set the dome across the top of the flower,
draw the bare wires together on the under
side, and twist hanging wires again.
d. Hook on a #16 stem wire. Close hook.
e. Thin out and shorten hanging wires and
tape down stem.
f. Tape 1 leaf 2″ under flower. Add a second
leaf 1″ under and a third 1″ below the second.

Shaping:

Flower petals stand up and out.
Leaves are pressed into the stem, and the
tips are bent back.

BLEEDING HEART

Materials

#25 gold wire
Pink and white crystal for flower
Medium green for foliage
Light green tape
#16 and #18 stem wire

Centers: White   Make a single 2½″ cross-over petal. Cut free from spool and spiral the beaded rows.   [10]

Petals: Pink   Split basic. Use a 6″ bottom basic loop.

        Basic 5   Pointed top
        Rows 9   and bottom   [10]
Work the bottom as follows: Before making the first pointed turn, bring the feed wire out to the side for 5 beads. Make a hairpin turn to form one side of a T. Make the pointed turn. Repeat the T-shape on the opposite side. Repeat this entire process on the other split petal.

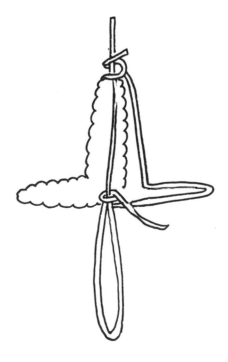

Buds: Pink on the wire, then add 2″ of white for each bud. Make a single 2″ cross-over petal. Cut free from spool and spiral the entire unit. [6]

Leaves: Split basic.

Basic 5	Pointed top
Rows 9	and bottom

Split the basic loop and make a petal as follows:

Basic 1″	Pointed top
Rows 5	and bottom

Cut away from spool, leaving 2″ of bare wire. Hold side by side and bend the tips outward. [8]

Assembly:

a. Set the heart units with petals facing each other, front sides out.

b. Insert the center unit between the petals. Twist the hanging wires.

c. Tape hanging wires of flowers and buds.

d. Tape a 6″ piece of **#18** stem wire.

e. Tape a leaf to the top, then add 3 more ½″ under one another, on opposite sides. Repeat for second leaf branch.

f. Tape a **#16** stem wire.

g. Tape a bud to the top with 1″ of stem showing.

h. Add the remaining buds ¼″ under one another, all with 1″ of stem showing.

i. Tape the hearts ¼″ down and ¼″ under one another, all with 1″ of stem showing.

j. Add the leaf branches 2″ under, on opposite sides.

Shaping:

The bottom tips of the heart are all bent outward.

The branch is bent into an arc.

All buds and hearts hang down.

One leaf branch is bent upward, the other is arched downward.

BLUE LACE FLOWER

Materials
#28 silver wire
#32 binding wire
Blue crystal
Dark green tape
#16 stem wire

Florets:
UNIT 1: 5–10-bead loops, all on one   [8]
        wire
        a. Twist the feed wire around the starting wire, pulling it snugly against the loops.
        b. Cut away the starting wire.
        c. Leave 1″ of beads on the feed wire for a stem and cut free from spool, leaving 3″ of bare wire.
UNIT 2: Same as Unit 1, but leave   [18]
        1½″ of beads for a stem

Assembly:
a. Join parts of Unit 1 into 2 groups of 4, by twisting the hanging wires together just under the beads.
b. Join parts of Unit 2 into groups of 3 the same way.
c. Tape the bare wires of each twisted group.
d. Tape a 12″ piece of stem wire.
e. Bind on a Unit 1 grouping to the top. Add the second grouping right next to it.
f. Tape the bindings.
g. Bind on the Unit 2 assemblies in the same way, directly under, and spaced evenly around stem.
h. Tape down entire stem.

Shaping:
Each floret is opened flat.
Stems of the inner florets are arched up and out, with the flower facing out.
Stems of the outer florets fan out like an umbrella.
There are no leaves because they fall off when the flower opens.

BOUGAINVILLAEA

Materials

#26 silver, #26 red, and #25 gold wire
Red crystal and yellow crystal for centers
White and red speckled chalk beads
Medium green for foliage
Light green tape
#16 stem wire

Centers: #25 gold	Yellow	5—6-bead loops, all on 1 wire. Cut free from spool, leaving 2″ of bare wire. String ½″ of green on each leg. Twist hanging wires. Spiral stem and set loops into a cluster.		[7]
Petals 1: #26 silver	Speckled chalk	Basic ½″ Rows 5	Pointed top and bottom	[14]
Petals 2: #26 red	Red	Basic ½″ Rows 7	Pointed top and bottom	[24]
Leaves: #26 silver		Basic ¾″ Rows 7	Pointed top and bottom	[14]

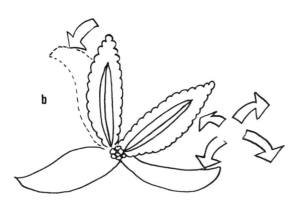

Assembly:

a. Hold 2 speckled petals together, face to face. Bend back the tips. Insert a center between them and twist the hanging wires.

b. Place 2 red petals together face up and 2 face down. Twist all hanging wires together. Open the 4 petals into a cross shape.

c. Set the speckled unit into the center. Twist all hanging wires again.

d. Press the 4 petals upward with the tips bent back. Tape the hanging stems.

e. Tape all leaf stems.

f. Tape a full length of #16 stem wire.

g. Tape the remaining speckled unit to the top of the stem with 1″ of stem exposed.

h. Tape on 2 leaves, opposite each other, 1″ below. Leaves have ½″ of stem showing.

i. Tape down, adding 1 flower and 2 leaves opposite each other, ¾″ under one another.

CAMELLIA

Materials

#26 silver wire for flower and leaves
#34 lacing wire
#32 binding wire
White, pink, or speckled chalk or crystal for
flower, plus a deeper color for outline
Dark green for foliage
Dark green tape
#16 stem wire

Center: Horizontal petals
     Basic ¾″   Keep round   [2]
     Rows 10
     Deepest color

Row 1: Basic 5   Round top   [6]
       Rows 9   Pointed bottom
       After Row 7, allow 6″ of bare wire and finish the last 2 rows in deepest
       color.

Row 2: Basic 5   Round top   [6]
       Rows 13   Pointed bottom
       After Row 11, allow 7″ of bare wire and finish the last 2 rows in deepest
       color. Decrease 1 bead on last 2 rows, to curl petal.

Row 3: Basic 10   Round top   [6]
       Rows 15   Pointed bottom
       After Row 13, allow 8″ of bare wire and finish the last 2 rows in
       deepest color. Decrease last 4 rows by 1 bead, to curl petal.

Calyx: Basic ¾″   Pointed top   [4]
      Rows 13   and bottom
      Lace through center.

Leaves: Basic 1″   Pointed top   [2]
      Rows 9   and bottom
      Rows 11   As above   [6]
      Lace the 11-row petals through center.

Assembly of Flower:

a. Place a pencil against the wrong side of each petal of center. Roll each petal around the pencil.

b. Insert one petal within another.

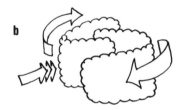

c. Twist the hanging wires 2 or 3 times.
d. Hook a **#16** stem through the wires.
e. Close hook.
f. Tape the hanging wires to the stem for ½", just under the beads.

g. With #32 wire, bind on each petal of Row 1, one at a time.
h. Cut away binding wire and tape under petals for ½".
i. Bind on the petals of Row 2 in the open spaces just below Row 1. Repeat g and h.
j. Bind on Row 3, repeating g, h, and i.
k. After all petals of Row 3 are bound on, tape down stem for 1".
l. Bind on the calyx one at a time, spacing them evenly around stem.
m. Cut away the binding wire. Thin out and shorten the hanging wires.
n. Tape down the entire stem.

Assembly of Leaf Stem:

a. Tape a piece of #16 stem wire.
b. Tape 1 small leaf at the top.
c. Follow illustration for spacing of leaves.

Assembly of Spray:

a. Attach leaf stem to flower stem with #32 wire, about 3" below flower head, with 2" of leaf *stem* extending beyond flower.
b. Cut away binding wire and tape down remainder of stem.

CANYON POPPY

Materials

#25 gold wire for centers, #26 silver for rest of parts
#32 binding wire
#34 lacing wire
Yellow and orange crystal for centers
White pearl for petals
Medium green for foliage
Dark green tape
#16 stem wire

Centers:	Yellow	4—1″ loops	[1]
		6—1½″ loops	[1]
	Orange	8—1¼″ loops	[1]
		10—1½″ loops	[1]
		8—1¾″ loops	[2]
		6—2″ loops	[3]
		Each set of loops is on one wire.	

Petals:		Basic 6	Round top	[6]
		Rows 21	Semipointed bottom	
		Lace each petal across center.		

Leaves:	Branch method*	Basic 2½″	Pointed top	[3]
		Rows 5	Round bottom	

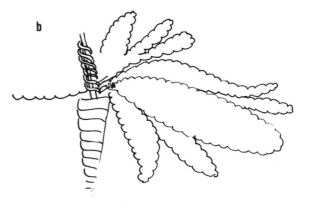

* 6″ loop on each side, then a 5½″ loop on each side, then a 5″ loop on each side. Continue with the feed wire and beads, and jewel for 1″. Lace ⅓ up from bottom.

Calyx:		5—2-inch 3-row crossovers, all on one wire [2]
Bud:	White	Basic 7 Both ends pointed [4]
		Rows 5
Bud Calyx:		6—2″ loops, all on one wire [1]

Assembly of Bud Stem:
a. Place bud calyx under bud. Press loops up and around bud.
b. Twist hanging wires 3 times and tape.
c. Tape a 6″ piece of #16 stem wire.
d. Tape bud to stem wire and jewel for 4″.

Assembly:
a. Set smaller yellow unit on top of larger.
b. Twist all wires together just under loops.
c. Hook a #16 stem through these 2 units. Close book.
d. Tape the third unit around the stem, directly underneath.
e. Bind on the next 2 units with #32 wire, evenly around stem.
f. Repeat until all centers are bound on, and tape for 1″.
g. Bind on the petals one at a time with #32 wire.
h. Taper and shorten the hanging wires.
i. Tape for 1″ under the flower.
j. Add calyx around stem with tape and push up gently against flower.

k. Tape down entire stem.
l. Add bud stem 2″ underneath, binding both stems together with #32 wire.
m. Tape on leaves ½″ under bud.
n. Continue adding leaves down stem 1″ under each other on opposite sides of the stem.
o. Jewel entire stem for 10″, starting directly under the flower head.

CATTAILS

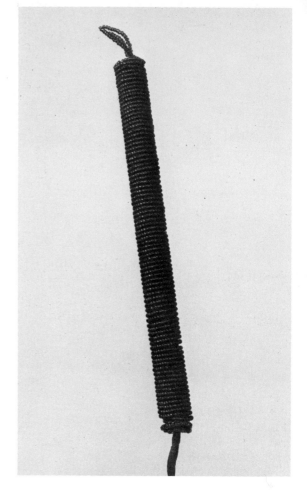

Materials

#32 silver wire
1 cardboard tube, taken from a wire clothes hanger, cut in half
Brown crystal
Dark green crystals
Brown tape
#16 stem wire

Leaf: With dark green
      Basic 1″   Pointed top
      Rows 3   and bottom   [1]

Cattail: With 5–40″ strands on the wire
      Basic 5   Round top
      Rows 8   and bottom   [2]
      Do not cut the basic wire.

Assembly:

a. Tape the leaf to the top of a stem wire.
b. Hold a brown circle over one end of the tube with bare wires hanging down the tube.
c. Tape these wires to the tube.
d. Repeat this on the opposite end of the tube.
e. Tape the entire tube.
f. Slip the stem through the tube, gently opening the center of the brown circles to allow it to fit. The leaf is the top.
g. Tape the tube in place with a few thicknesses of tape just under the tube.
h. Tape 2″ of bare feed wire to the top of the tube and "jewel" the entire tube.
i. Cut free from spool with 3″ of free wire.
j. String this wire through the center of the bottom petal and twist around the stem.
k. Tape the twist and tape down.

CHINESE HAT PLANT

Materials

#24 gold wire for hat
#25 gold wire for centers
#26 silver wire for leaves
#32 binding wire
Orange crystal for centers
Light green crystal for flower
Dark green for leaves
Light green tape
#16 stem wire

Each cluster has 7 flowers and 2 leaves.

Center: Orange   Start with 3″ of bare wire. Make the following loops all on one wire: ⅝″, ⅞″, 1⅛″, ⅞″, ⅝″. End with 3″ of bare wire. String 1″ of orange on to each hanging wire and twist the stems together. Spiral the 1″ of beads. Set 4 loops face up and the long loop bent down.

Flower "Hat": Light green Cut 4 pieces of #26 silver wire into 5″ lengths. Twist together

for 3″. Fan out to form a cross. Anchor the feed wire around the twisted stem and have it come up one leg for one twist. Use each leg for a basic turn and set 3 beads between each as you work around the frame. Work around for 7 rows. Cut all top wires and bend them back as top basics.

Leaves: Basic 1″   Pointed top   [2]
                Rows 13   and bottom

Assembly:

a. Set the center into the hat with the beaded stem sitting above the hat. Twist the bare wires and tape.

b. Tape a #16 stem wire.

c. Bind the flowers to the top in a cluster with 1¾″ of stem showing.

d. Tape the bindings.

e. Tape a 6″ piece of stem wire and tape the 2 leaves to the top, opposite one another.

f. Jewel the leaf stem for 3″.

g. Jewel the flower stem for 4″.

h. Tape the leaf stem to the main stem and continue with the jeweling for 4″ more.

i. Tape the end wires of the jeweling, then tape down remainder of stem.

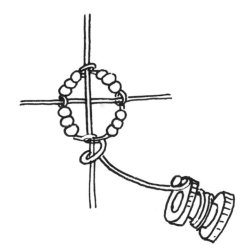

CHRYSANTHEMUM, ANEMONE

Materials

#25 gold and #26 silver wire
#32 binding wire
#34 lacing wire
Light and dark orange crystal for flower
Dark green and a small amount of light green
for foliage
Dark green tape
#16 stem wire

Center: #25 gold	Darker shade	10—2½″ loops, all on one wire	[2]
Petals: #25 gold ROW 1:		Basic 12 Pointed top Rows 7* and bottom * After completing 5 rows, estimate enough wire to complete petal. Cut away from spool and string lighter shade on cut end. Finish petal.	[7]
ROW 2:	Split basic	Basic 1½″ Pointed top Rows 3 and bottom	[6]
ROW 3:	Split basic	Add lighter shade for basic count. Basic 2″ Pointed top Rows 3 and bottom	[9]
Calyx:	Dark green	2″ loop, 3″ loop, 2″ loop, all on one wire	[4]
Leaves:	*Branch method	String dark green on wire, adding 3″ of light green at random. Basic 2″ Pointed top Rows 5* and bottom * After fifth row is completed, add 2 loops on each side, 5½″. Tape hanging wires of each leaf and jewel for 1″.	[3]

Assembly:

a. Twist hanging wires of center units for ½″.

b. Hook on a #16 stem wire. Close hook and tape for 1″.

c. Bind on the first row, one petal at a time, to fit evenly around stem.

d. Tape the bindings.

e. Bind on the second row in the same manner.

f. Bind on the final row the same way.

g. Narrow the loops of the calyx and bind them on one at a time, just under the flower.

h. Cut away binding wire. Taper and shorten all hanging wires.

i. Tape down the remainder of the stem.

j. Bind on the leaves with #32 wire one at a time 2″ under the flower. Space them evenly around, all facing the stem.

Shaping:

All loops of center are set straight up and overlapping.

Row 1 petals point straight out horizontally.

Row 2 petals point out with tips curved toward the center.

Row 3 petals have half the petal curving downward.

The short loop of the calyx is pressed up into the flower, while the long loop curves downward.

Two leaves face the stem, and the front leaf is curled down.

CHRYSANTHEMUM, ANNUAL

Materials

#25 gold wire
#32 binding wire
Orange or yellow crystal for main color
Topaz and brown crystal for contrast
Light green for foliage
Light green tape
#16 stem wire

Centers:	Topaz	7—1″ loops, all on one wire	[1]
	Brown	7—1½″ loops, all on one wire	[2]

Petals: String as follows for each petal: ½″ of topaz, 1½″ of main color, ⅞″ of topaz, ⅞″ of main color, 10 topaz beads, 12 beads in main color, 11 topaz beads.

Basic 7	Round top	[8]
Rows 7	Pointed bottom	

Leaves: *Branch method [2]
   a. Knot the end of the wire, allow 3″ of bare wire, then measure 1″ of beads.
   b. Let the 1″ float freely out of the way and make 3—1½″ loops.
   c. Measure 1″ of beads to match the first 1″. Twist the bare wire to lock the beads securely in place. Spiral.
   d. * Make two 2″ loops on each side of this point.

Calyx: 6—1½″ loops with 2 beads between each loop, all on one wire. Narrow the loops.

Assembly:

a. Tape a 10″ piece of stem wire and bind on the topaz center.
b. Add the brown centers, one on each side of the stem, just under the topaz. Tape for ½″.
c. Bind on the petals one at a time to fit evenly around stem.
d. Cut away binding wire, shorten and taper the hanging wires. Tape for 1″.
e. Add the calyx and tape down entire stem.
f. Add the leaves 2″ under the flower, opposite each other.

CHRYSANTHEMUM, SPIDER

Materials

#25 gold or #26 silver wire; 2 spools are needed
#32 binding wire
Any two harmonizing colors in crystal
Dark green for foliage
Dark green tape
#16 stem wire

String each color on a separate spool.

Unit 1: Hold both wires together and measure each loop together. 3—1″ loops, all on one wire. Spiral each double loop. [1]

Unit 2: As above.
6—1½″ loops, all on one wire [1]

Unit 3: Measure the darker loop first. Measure the light loop. Set the dark loop over the light loop and spiral them together. Pinch the extended tip of the light loop. [3]
Dark loops: 4—1½″ loops
Light loops: 4—2″ loops

43

Unit 4:	Same method.	[4]
	Dark loops:3—2½″ loops	
	Light loops: 3—3″ loops	

Unit 5:	Same method	[3]
	Dark loops: 6—3½″ loops	
	Light loops: 6—4″ loops	

| **Calyx:** | 9—2″ loops, all on one wire | [2] |

| **Leaves:** | The following sizes are crossovers, all on one wire: 2″, 2½″, 3½″, 2½″, 2″. | [5] |

Assembly:

a. Twist the hanging wires of Unit 1 together.

b. Hook a #16 stem wire through. Close hook.

c. Bind on Unit 2. Tape for ½″.

d. Bind on Unit 3 one at a time to fit evenly around stem.

e. Tape the binding for ½″.

f. Bind on each succeeding unit, closely under the previous one. Tape for ½″ after each binding is completed.

g. Bind on the calyx, one on each side of the stem, closely under that flower head.

h. Thin and taper the hanging wires and tape down entire stem.

i. Tape the hanging wires of each leaf.

j. Add the leaves 2″ under the flower and 1″ under each other, on alternate sides of the stem.

k. Tape down remainder of stem.

Shaping:

All loops are curved slightly up and out.

The leaves are alternately shaped up and down.

CHRYSANTHEMUM, SPOON

Materials

#25 gold wire for flower
#26 silver wire for foliage
#32 binding wire
Light yellow crystal for centers
Deeper yellow crystal for petals
Medium green for foliage
Dark green tape
Stem beads
#16 and #20 stem wire

| **Center 1:** | 6—1½″ loops, all on one wire | [5] |

| **Center 2:** | 8—1½″ loops, all on one wire | [2] |

Petals:

ROW 1:   5—double 5″ loops, all on one
wire   [4]
Procedure:
a. Make a 5″ loop.
b. Make a ½″ loop at the top
of this by twisting beads
once.

b

c. Start a second loop, but go
around the twisted portion as
a basic turn.

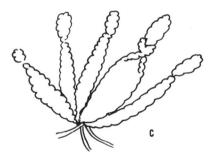

c

d. Set the loops on top of one
another.

ROW 2:   Repeat the above method with:

Bud: 5—double 5½″ loops   [4]

Dark: 6—1½″ loops, all on one wire [1]

Light: 4—1½″ loops, all on one wire [1]

**Bud
Calyx:**   8—1″ loops, all on one wire [1]

**Flower
Calyx:**   9—2″ loops, all on one wire [2]

Leaves: [2]

a. Tape 1″ of one end of an 8″ piece of #20
stem wire.
b. String 3″ of stem beads on to wire.
c. Tape the bare stem closely under the stem
beads.
d. Anchor the feed wire under the stem
beads.
e. Tape exposed wire.
f. Work 7 rows in all. Pointed top and bottom.
g. Make 2–6″ crossover petals on each side.
h. Continue with the beads on the feed wire
and jewel the leaf stem for 1″.

Assembly of Flower:

a. Place two units of Center 1 on top of one
another and twist the hanging wires.
b. Hook a #16 stem through. Close hook.
c. Bind on the remainder of Center 1, one
unit at a time, to fit around.
d. Bind on Center 2 in the same manner.
e. Bind on the small petal units in the same
manner. Tape the binding.
f. Bind on the larger petals. Tape bindings.
g. Form calyx into a circle. Place firmly under the flower and bind on.
h. Taper and cut all hanging wires.
i. Tape down remainder of stem.

Assembly of Bud:

a. Cluster the yellow loops straight up.
b. Set the lighter loops around the darker
and twist hanging wires.
c. Set bud calyx firmly in place and twist
hanging wires again.
d. Tape to a 4″ piece of #20 stem.
e. Jewel the stem for 2″.

Assembly of Flower Stem:

a. Jewel the flower stem for 2½″.
b. Add the bud stem with binding wire, tape
together, and jewel for 1½″.
c. Add a leaf with binding wire, opposite
the bud, tape, and jewel for 1″.
d. Add a leaf on the back of the stem and
jewel for 2″.
e. Tape down remainder of stem.

Shaping:

Centers are clustered in a ball shape.
Petals are slightly angled up and out.
Leaves are faced up with tips bent back.

CINERARIA

Materials
#28 silver for flower
#26 silver for foliage
Yellow for centers
Blue, red, pink, white, or purple for flower
Dark green tape
#18 stem wire

Each spray has 4 flowers and 3 leaves.

Petals:	10—1½″ loops, all on one wire [1]
Centers:	8-bead loop wrapped once [1]
Leaves:	*Branch method

Leaves: *Branch method
Basic ½″   Semipointed top, [3]
Rows 11   round bottom
* 3¼″ loop on each side, then
2¾″ loop on each side

Assembly of Flower:
a. Narrow the loops of the petals.
b. Bring end wire across to beginning of petal. Weave end wire in and out among the loops, halfway around the petal, to close circle.
c. Bring one end wire of the center unit across the underside of the petals. Go up, over, and down across the center bead of the outer loop.
d. Straddle center across flower. Bring all wires together at the underside. Twist securely and tape.
e. Close loops of the leaves tightly and press, following the shape of the petal.
f. Tape hanging wires of leaves.

Assembly of Spray:
a. Tape one flower to the top of a 12″ piece of stem wire; ¾″ of flower stem shows.
b. Add 3 more flowers ¼″ below, evenly around stem.
c. Tape one leaf 2″ under flower with ¼″ of stem showing.
d. Add 2 more leaves ¼″ below, opposite one another.

Shaping:
All petals are gently pressed up at the centers and arched out.
Flowers face forward. Leaves parallel floor.

CLEMATIS

Materials

#26 silver and #25 gold wire
#32 binding wire
Two shades of any color in crystal
Dark and light green
Dark green tape
#16 and #20 stem wire

Center 1: #25 gold	Dark green	6–1" loops, all on one wire	[1]
Center 2:* #25 gold	Light green	¾" *Single beaded stems, Method II	[4]
Petals: #26 silver	With light shade on the wire, add 1¾" of dark for each petal.		
		Basic ½" Round top	[7]
		Rows 7 Semipointed bottom	
Leaves: #26 silver	String dark and light green at random.		
		Basic ½" Pointed top	[2 per flower]
		Rows 9 Round bottom	

Trim off the entire basic loop, leaving ½" to bend to back of the leaf. Leave 3" of beads on the feed wire and cut away from spool, leaving 2" of bare wire.

Assembly of Flower:

a. Cut 3–4" pieces of #20 stem wire. Tape each one.
b. Tape Center 1 to the top of the stem.
c. Tape Center 2 just under, and evenly spaced around 1.
d. Bind on the 7 petals one at a time to fit evenly around.
e. Cut away binding wire and taper the hanging wires.
f. Tape down remainder of stem.
Repeat the above process for 2 more flowers (3 in all).

Assembly of Branch:

a. Twist the bare wires of 2 leaves together.

Spiral the beaded stem around a pencil. Repeat for all leaves.
b. Tape a #16 stem wire.
c. Tape a leaf assembly to the top.
d. Tape a flower stem 1" under with 2" of flower stem showing beyond the main stem.
e. Add a leaf assembly and a flower, 1" under one another, in the same manner until all units are attached.
f. Tape down the remainder of the stem.

Shaping:

The center spiraled stems stand straight up.
The petals stand out horizonatally.
The flower stems are bent to face forward and slightly angled to the side of the main stem.
The leaves go in any direction, very casually.

COLEUS

Materials
#26 silver wire
Combinations in crystal of 2 shades of red; or pink and green; orange and yellow; red and pink; red and light green; 2 shades of yellow
Dark green tape
#18 stem wire

String the darker color on the wire. Add the lighter shade for the basic amounts. Complete all but the final 2 rows and estimate enough wire to finish the last 2 rows. Cut free from spool and string the lighter shade on to complete petal.

Row 1: Basic 5   Pointed top and bottom on all petals   [2]
         Rows 7

Row 2: Basic 7   As above   [2]
         Rows 9

Row 3: Basic 10   As above   [2]
         Rows 9

Row 4: Basic 10   As above   [6]
         Rows 11

Assembly:
a. Tape a #18 stem wire.
b. Tape the first 2 petals to the top, facing each other.
c. Tape on each set of petals ¼" under one another, facing each other, alternating direction as you tape down the stem. Pairs will face north and south, then east and west, etc.
d. The last 6 petals are treated as though they were pairs.

Shaping:
The bottoms of the petals hug the stem.
All petals stand out horizontally.

COLUMBINE

Materials

#25 gold or #26 silver wire
#32 binding wire
Yellow crystal for the centers
Any two shades of crystal to blend or contrast
Light green for foliage
Dark green tape
#16 stem wire

Centers:		9–2½″ loops plus a 3″ loop, all on one wire		[1]
Inner Petals:	Light color	Basic 4	Round top	[5]
		Rows 13	Pointed bottom	
	Work tightly at the top, to curl petal.			
Outer Petals:	Dark color	Basic ¾″	Pointed top	[5]
		Rows 11	and bottom	
	End each petal with a 4½″ bead loop.			
	Set loop tightly against bottom of petal.			
Leaves:		Basic 1¼″	Pointed top	[2]
		Rows 11	Round bottom	[2]
		Rows 13	As above	

Assembly:

a. Spiral each loop of the center unit and close them into a circle. The tallest loop stands up in the center of the circle.

b. Twist the hanging wires and hook the stem wire through. Close hook.

c. Bind on the inner petals to fit evenly around.

d. Tape the bindings.

e. Spiral the "tails" of the outer petals and have them hang down with the bottom tips bent out. Bind on the petals to fit evenly around the stem.

f. Taper and cut all hanging wires.

g. Tape down entire stem.

h. Add 2 small leaves 2″ under the flower, opposite each other.

i. Add the 2 larger leaves 2″ under, in the same manner.

CUP OF GOLD

Materials

#25 gold wire
#32 binding wire
Yellow, brown, and white crystal
Medium green for foliage
Light green tape
#16 and #18 stem wire

Centers:	Yellow. Add 8 white beads for each stamen 8-bead loop. Trim the starting wire close to the beads, push over 1″ of yellow, and cut wire away from spool, leaving 2″ of bare wire. [6]		
Bud:*	Yellow	Basic 5	Pointed top [4]
		Rows 5	Round bottom
	* Do not cut away basic wires. Lantern assembly.		
Petals:	Yellow on wire, then add 1″ of brown for each petal.		
		Basic 1″	Round top [6]
		Rows 9	and bottom
Bud Leaves:		Basic ¾″	Pointed top [1]
		Rows 5	and bottom [2]
		Rows 7	
Flower Leaves:		Basic ¾″	Pointed top [3]
		Rows 9	and bottom

Assembly:

a. Assemble the bud petals in a lantern assembly. Tape the hanging wires for 2″.
b. Twist the bare wires of the bud leaves together, shape them into a fan, and tape for 2″. Do the same with the flower leaves.
c. Tape a 4″ piece of #18 stem wire.
d. Tape the bud to the top, add the leaves 1″ under with 1″ of stem showing.
e. Tape a #16 stem wire.
f. Tape the centers to the top.
g. Bind on the petals with #32 wire one at a time, to fit evenly around stem.

h. Taper and cut all hanging wires.
i. Tape down the entire stem.
j. Add the bud branch 2″ under the flower. Bind and tape.
k. Add the flower leaves 1″ under the bud branch, on the opposite side, with 1″ of stem showing.

Shaping:

Petals are shaped like a bell. The bottoms stand out horizontally, and the remainder of the petal is bent up.
Leaves stand straight out.

CUPID'S-DART

Materials
#26 silver wire
#32 binding wire
Yellow chalk or crystal for center loops
Red crystal for center dome
Dark blue crystal for petals
Dark green for foliage
Dark green tape
#16 stem wire

Center 1:	Basic 5　Dome petal	[1]
	Rows 10	
Center 2:	8–2″ loops, all on one wire	[1]
Petals:	4–2¾″ 4-row crossovers, all on one wire	[2]
	4–4″, as above	[4]
Calyx:	6–1½″ loops, all on one wire	[2]
Leaves:	3–3″ 4-row crossovers, all on 1 wire, with 2 beads between petals	
	3–5″, as above	[3]

Assembly:
a. Bring the hanging wires of the dome together under the back.
b. Set Center 2 loops all around the dome. Twist all hanging wires.
c. Hook a #16 stem through and close hook.
d. Tape for ½″.
e. Bind on the small petal units with one on each side of the stem.
f. Bind on the larger petal units one at a time to fit evenly around.
g. Tape down stem.
h. Tape the small leaves 3″ down, opposite each other.
i. Tape the larger leaves 1″ under, spaced evenly around stem.
j. Tape down remainder of stem.

CYCLAMEN

Materials

#26 gold wire for center, #25 gold wire for remainder of flower
#32 binding wire
Yellow crystal for centers
Raspberry crystal for petals
Dark and light green for foliage
Brown tape
#16 and #18 stem wire

Center:	3—10-bead loops, all on one wire		[1]
Petals:	Basic ¾″	Round top	[7]
	Rows 15	Semipointed bottom	
	Work tightly to curl petal.		
Calyx:	4—8-bead loops wrapped once with 3 beads between sections, all on one wire		[1]
Leaves:	String dark and add 2″ of light, at random.		
	Basic 10	Pointed top	[2]
	Rows 18	Round bottom	

*V split:
* Open the basic loop after the seventh row. Work as a V split until 18 rows are completed. String 7 beads on to each leg of the V and draw each one through to the back of the petal. Join all wires and twist together.

Assembly:

a. Tape a #16 stem wire.
b. Tape the center to the top.
c. Bind on each petal, with front of petal facing the stem wire, evenly around stem.
d. Bind on the calyx just under the flower. Smaller loop is pressed into the flower, the larger loop stands away.
e. Thin out and taper hanging wires. Tape down stem.
f. Tape each leaf to a separate piece of #18 stem wire, 5″ long.
g. Tape the leaf stems to the bottom of the flower stem, one on each side.

Shaping:

With pliers, bend the flower stem into a hairpin curve, just under the calyx.
Bring 5 petals upward, and 2 hang down. Make sure all petals show their front sides out.

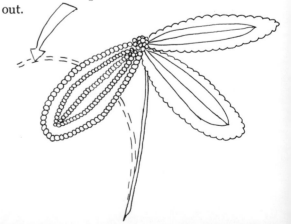

DAHLIA, ANNUAL

Materials

#26 and #28 silver wire
#32 binding wire
Black and yellow crystal or chalk for centers
Any color crystal or cut crystal for petals
Medium green for foliage
Dark green tape
#16 stem wire

Petals:		Basic ¾″	Semipointed	[8]
#26		Rows 9	top and bottom	
Centers:	Black 1	6—10-bead loops, all on one wire		[1]
#28	Black 2	8—1″ loops, all on one wire		[1]
	Yellow	10—1⅝″ loops, all on one wire		[1]
Calyx:		4—2½″ loops, 4-row crossovers with 4 beads be-		
#28		tween loops.		[1]
Leaves:		Basic 9	Pointed top	[3]
#26		Rows 7	and bottom	
		Basic 12	As above	[3]
		Rows 9		

Assembly:

a. Form Center 1 into a cluster.

b. Set Center 2 under 1 and twist hanging wires twice.

c. Set yellow center just below and twist again.

d. Hook a #16 stem wire, 10″ long, through centers.

e. Close hook and tape for ½″.

f. With #32 wire, bind on petals one at a time, directly under the center. (Petals overlap slightly.)

g. Thin out and taper hanging wires to 1½″.

h. Bind on the calyx in the same manner and tape the entire stem.

i. Tape on the smaller leaves 2″ below the flower in a triangular position.

j. Tape on the larger leaves 1″ below the smaller in the same manner.

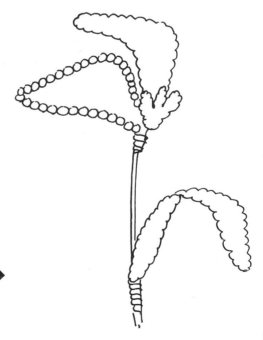

DAHLIA, CACTUS

Materials

#25 gold wire
#32 binding wire
Two shades of any color crystal
Light green for foliage
Light green tape
#16 stem wire

Center: Light color   3—1¼″ 4-row cross-
                              overs, all on one
                              wire   [1]

Make the crossover loop very loose and
spiral the entire unit.

Petals: Light color

Procedure: Press loop Number 1 gently
closed before crossing over. Loop Number 2
(the crossover loop) is longer. Both loops are
spiraled together, and the remainder of the
longer loop is pressed flat.

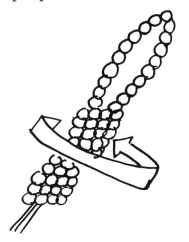

ROW 1:   3—4-row crossovers,
                    all on one wire [3]
Loop 1 is 1″ long. Crossover loop is 2″ long.
ROW 2:   Repeat above.   [4]
ROW 3:   Dark color   4—4-row crossovers,
                      all on one wire [3]
Loop 1 is 2½″ long. Crossover loop is 3½″
long.
ROW 4:   Dark color   [4]
Leave 8″ of bare wire. Make a single 2¾″
loop. On the same wire, make 2 crossover sec-
tions as follows: Loop 1 is 2¾″ long. Cross-
over loop is 3¾″ long. Right next to this make

a single loop 2¾″ long. Cut away 8″ of bare
wire. String the light color on the first 8″
hanging wire, and the final 8″ hanging wire.
Complete a crossover on each single loop,
measuring 3¾″. This will give you 4 crossover petals, 2 of which are solid color, 2 are
double color. Spiral the petals.

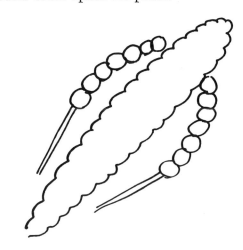

ROW 5:   Use the same procedure as
         Row 4.   [5]
Loop 1 is 2¾″ long. Crossover loop is 4″
long.

Calyx: 2″ loop, 3″ loop, 2″ loop, all
             on one wire   [4]

Leaves: Basic 1″   Pointed top [3]
             Rows 11   and bottom

Assembly:

a. Twist the hanging wires of the center.
b. Hook a #16 stem wire through. Close
hook.

c. Bind on Row 1 units one at time with
#32 wire. Space evenly around.
d. Cut away binding wire and tape for ½″.
e. Bind on each row in the same manner.
f. Bind on the calyx one at a time and tape
down entire stem.
g. Tape the leaves 2″ under the flower in a
triangular position.

Shaping:

The flower tips all stand out straight.
The calyx has the long loop bent down and
the short loop pressing against the flower.

DAHLIA, FOREST FIRE

Materials

#25 gold wire
#32 binding wire
Yellow and red crystal for flower
Medium green for foliage
Dark green tape
#16 stem wire

Petals:

ROW 1:   String as follows for each petal:
          ⅝″ yellow, ¾″ red, ⅝″ yellow, 5 red beads.
                         Basic 10   Pointed top   [3]
                         Rows 3   and bottom

ROW 2:   String as follows for each petal:
          ⅝″ yellow, 1½″ red, ⅞″ yellow, ¾″ red, ⅝″ yellow, 5 red beads.
                         Basic 10   Pointed top   [5]
                         Rows 5   and bottom

ROW 3:   String as follows for each petal:
          4½″ red, ⅞″ yellow, ½″ red, 1¼″ yellow, 1¾″ red, 10 yellow beads.
                         Basic 10   Pointed top   [11]
                         Rows 7   and bottom

Leaves: Basic 10   Pointed top   [4]
                         Rows 9   and bottom

Calyx: 1″ loop, 2″ loop, 1″ loop, 2″ loop, all on one wire [3]

Assembly:

a. Tape a 10″ piece of #16 stem wire.

b. With the *wrong* side up, bind on the petals of Row 1 with #32 wire, forming a triangle.

c. With the *wrong* side up, bind on each petal of Row 2. Tape for ½″.

d. With the *wrong* side up, do the same with 5 petals of Row 3.

e. With the right side up, bind on the remaining 6 petals of Row 3.

f. Cut away the binding wire and tape down for 1″.

g. Add the calyx to the back of the flower, binding them on to form a circle around the stem.

h. Thin out and taper the hanging wires, and tape down remainder of stem.

i. Tape the leaf stems and add them to the main stem 1″ under the flower and 1″ under and opposite each other; ½″ of leaf stem shows.

Shaping:

The 3 center petals are shaped as a lantern with the tips touching. Pull them gently up into a peak.

The next row of petals is arched up with the tips bent toward the center.

The next row of 5 petals has a wider arc with the tips toward the center.

The final row of petals stands straight out horizontally with the tips bent back.

The short loops of the calyx are pressed up into the flower, the long loops are bent down.

The leaves stick out almost straight from the stem.

DAHLIA, GIANT
CACTUS SPRAY

Materials
#24 or #25 gold wire for flower parts
#26 silver wire for all foliage
#32 binding wire
Any 3 or 4 shades of warm color in crystal
Medium green for foliage
Dark green tape
#16 and #14 stem wire

Each section has its own assembly. All jeweling is done with the binding wire. All sections are connected with binding wire and then taped.

Section 1: Leaf Branch

LEAF 1:	Basic ½″ Rows 17	Both ends pointed	[2]
LEAF 2:	Basic ½″ Rows 19	Both ends pointed	[2]
"TRIO"	Lace through center and brace down back.		
LEAF 3:	Basic ¾″ Rows 25	Both ends pointed	[1]

◀ Lace through center and brace down back. Add a 2″ beaded loop under bottom of leaf.

Assembly:

◀ a. Leaves 1 are taped to the top of a #16 stem wire, face to face. Jewel stem for 7½″.
b. Leaves 2 and 3 are put on to their own stem, and throughout the rest of the design will be referred to as a "trio" branch. The larger leaf goes between the 2 smaller ones, with the bottom of the 2″ beaded loop coming even with the bottom of the 2 smaller leaves. Jewel for 1½″.
c. Join stem 1 and trio stem where the jeweling ends, and jewel together for 3″.

Section 2: Bud

ROW 1:	5–1½" loops		[1]
ROW 2:	6–2" loops, 3-row crossovers		[1]
CALYX:	Basic ½" Rows 5	Pointed top Round bottom	[5]
BUD LEAVES:	Basic ½"	Both ends pointed	[2]
PLUS A LEAF "TRIO"	Rows 17		

Assembly:

a. Join loops of each row by twisting hanging wires together.

b. Fit loops of Row 2 around under Row 1.

c. Tape a #16 stem wire and tape the loops to the top.

d. Add the calyx, binding on one at a time with #32 wire, spacing evenly around under the bud.

e. Shorten the hanging wires and tape down entire stem.

f. Jewel the bud stem for 4½". Add 1 leaf on each side, then jewel for another 4".

g. Add a "trio" branch and jewel this for 1½".

h. Add the "trio" to the bud stem and jewel together for 3".

Section 3: Small Flower

CENTER:	Basic 4 Rows 10	Dome petal Keep round	[1]
PETALS	Basic 1½" Rows 5	Pointed top Round bottom	[7]
ROW 1: light color			
ROW 2: medium color	As above		[8]
ROW 3: dark color	As above		[13]
CALYX:	22–3" loops, all on one wire		[1]

Lace ⅓ of the way down. Jewel stem for 7". Add a leaf trio (trio stem is jeweled for 1½"). Add trio to flower stem and jewel together for 4½".

Assembly:

a. Join hanging wires of dome petal, twist securely.

b. Hook on a #14 stem wire. Close the hook.

c. Tape for ½".

d. Bind on one petal at a time with #32 wire, spacing evenly around the stem. Cut away binding wire and tape down for ¾".

e. Bind on the next row the same way. Bind on the third row same way.

f. Tape down the entire stem.

g. Form the calyx into a circle by bringing the ending wire over to starting point and going in and out around the base, halfway around, until one wire hangs down each side.

h. Bind on the calyx with #32. Shorten the hanging wires.

i. Tape the exposed wire.

j. Jewel for the number of inches already specified.

Section 4: Larger Flower

Make 2 of this size.

CENTER:	Basic 4	Dome petal	[1]
	Rows 10	Very round	
PETALS:	Basic 1½″	Pointed top	[7]
ROW 1: light color	Rows 5	Round bottom	
ROW 2: medium color	As above		[8]
ROW 3: dark color	As above		[13]
ROW 4: darker color	As above		[17]

Assembly:

Follow Section 3. One flower stem is jeweled 8″. Add a leaf trio (trio stem is jeweled for 1½″). Jewel the two stems together for 4½″. Second flower is jeweled 9″. Leaf trio is jeweled for 2″. Jewel the 2 stems together for 4½″.

Assembly of Entire Spray:

a. Join the sections together with binding wire and tape.
b. All sections are joined wherever the jeweling ends.

For an entire spray you will need the following count:

PETALS COLOR	#1		21
	#2		24
	#3		39
	#4		34
LEAVES SIZE	17 row		4
	19 row		10
	25 row		5
CALYX	all same size		3

DAISY, DOUBLE-PAINTED

Materials
#26 and #28 silver wire
#32 binding wire
Yellow for centers
Two harmonizing colors for the flower in crystal, cut crystal, or iridescent.
Any green for foliage
Green tape to blend with foliage
Stem beads
#20 stem wire

Center:	3–1⅛″ loops, all on one wire	[1]
Row 1:	6–1½″ loops, all on one wire, in lighter color	
Row 2:	9–2″ loops, all on one wire, in darker color	
	Top of each loop is given a half-twist, to form a tiny circle.	
Row 3:	9–2″ 4-row crossovers, all on one wire, in lighter color	[1]
Bud:	1–1¼″ loop in yellow	[1]
	5–1½″ loops, all on one wire, in darker color	
	7–1¾″ loops, all on 1 wire, in lighter color	
Bud Calyx:	3–1¾″ loops, all on 1 wire	
	Top of each loop is given a half-twist, to form a tiny circle.	
Leaves:	Basic 2″ Pointed top	[9]
	Rows 5 Round bottom	

Assembly:
a. Form center of flower into a circle.
b. Hook a #20 stem wire through and close hook.
c. Form Row 1 into a circle. Slide on to the stem and tape to stem for ½″.
d. Form Row 2 into a circle. Slide on to stem and bind tightly.
e. Bind on Row 3, cut away binding wire, and trim all hanging wires to ¾″.
f. Tape for ¾″ only.
g. Jewel for ¾″. End jeweling securely, just under beads.

h. Push stem beads on to stem in the amount suggested below.
i. Tape under stem beads, catching last bead into tape, to hold securely.

For a spray of 3 flowers, 9 leaves and 2 buds:
Flower stems: 5½″, 4¾″, 4¼″.
Bud stem: 3½″, 4″. (Second bud stem is optional.)
Leaf stems: 4 stems are beaded for 1½″.
5 stems remain taped only.

Assembly of Bud:
Assemble like flower, but add the bud calyx as a final row.

Assembly of Spray:
a. After all parts are assembled individually, join one unit to another where the stem beads end and bind together, then tape together.
b. All leaves are joined in the same position at the base of the flower, evenly spaced around the stem.
c. Stand the beaded ones up tall, between the taped ones.

DAISY, FIELD

Materials
#28 silver wire
#32 binding wire
White and yellow chalk for flower
Dark green for foliage
Dark green tape
#16 stem wire

Center:	Yellow	Basic 5	Round top	[1]
		Rows 8	and bottom	

Ending is at the *top* basic. Do not cut away any basic wires.

Petals:	White	4—2″ loops, all on one wire	[4]
Leaves:		Individual 4″ loop	[3]

Cut free from spool, and spiral.

Assembly:
a. Tape a #16 stem wire.
b. Bind on the petal units to the top. Space them evenly around stem.
c. Set the center unit across the top and bring the end wires down along the stem.
d. Taper and shorten the hanging wires.
e. Tape down the entire stem.
f. Add the leaves 1″ under the flower, then 1″ under one another.

Shaping:
The flower petals stand straight out.
The leaves curl away from the stem.

DAISY, SHASTA

Materials
#26 silver and #25 gold wire for center
#32 binding wire
White crystal or chalk with yellow for center
Light and dark green for foliage
Dark green tape
#16 stem wire

Center:		7–1½″ loops, all on one wire	[1]
Petals:			
ROW 1:		10–1½″ loops, all on one wire	[3]
ROW 2:		16–2″ loops, all on one wire	[1]
ROW 3:		Repeat Row 2.	[1]
ROW 4:		10–4″ loops, all on one wire	[3]
Calyx:	Dark green	8–2″ loops, all on one wire	[1]
Leaves:	Dark green on wire; add 3″ light for each leaf.		
		Basic 3″ Pointed top	[6]
		Rows 3 and bottom	

Assembly:
a. cluster the center loops, all face up.
b. Hook a #16 stem through. Close the hook.
c. Bind on the first row to fit evenly around. Tape bindings.
d. Repeat for the next 3 rows.
e. Thin out and taper the hanging wires.
f. Tape down entire stem.
g. Tape 3 leaves to stem one at a time, 4″ under flower.
h. Tape each of the remaining 3 leaves 1½″ below.

Shaping:
Center loops stand straight up.
Rows 1 and 2 are at an angle to stem.
Rows 3 and 4 are horizontal to stem.
Calyx is pressed up into flower.
Leaves stand upright with tips curled outward.

DESERT ROSE

Materials
#25 gold and #26 silver wire
#32 binding wire
Topaz and brown crystal for flower
Dark green for foliage
Brown tape
#16 and #18 stem wire

Inner petals: #25	Topaz	Basic 9 Rows 5	Pointed top and bottom	[4]
Outer petals: #25	Topaz with a few brown at random spots	Basic ¾″ Rows 13*	Round top and bottom	[5]
		* After eleventh row, estimate enough free wire to complete 2 more rows. Cut away from spool and string on brown to finish petal.		
Leaves: #26		Basic 9 Rows 9	Pointed top Round bottom	[3]
Calyx: #26		12—2″ loops, all on one wire		[1]

Assembly:
a. Twist the hanging wires of the inner petals together.
b. Fan out petals so all fronts face up.
c. Hook a #16 stem through and close hook.
d. Bind on the outer row with #32 wire, spacing evenly around.
e. Cut away binding wire and tape for ½″.
f. Add calyx closely under flower head and bind on with #32.
g. Trim all hanging wires and tape down stem.

h. Tape a 6″ piece of #18 stem wire, tape a leaf to the top.
i. Tape another leaf 1″ under and add a third opposite.
j. Tape remainder of stem and add this branch 2″ under the flower with 4″ of branch showing.

Shaping:
Inner petals are horizontal with tips bent back.
Outer petals follow this shape also.

DOGWOOD BRANCH

Materials

#26 silver wire for flowers and foliage

#32 binding wire

Pink with brown trim or white with green trim in crystal

Medium green for foliage

Brown tape

#16 stem wire

For each branch make 2 flowers of 1, 2, and 3. Make 1 of 4.

Flower 1: Basic 4   Round top   [4]
Rows 7   Pointed bottom
String 5 beads in trim color on top basic wire. Bring down to front of petal for 2 or 3 rows. String through to back of petal. Catch the open end of the top basic through the ridges on the back of the petal. Pull securely and cut away excess wire.

Flower 2: Basic 4   *Round top   [4]
Rows 11   Pointed bottom
* V split at seventh row. String 6 beads in trim color on to each leg of V.

Flower 3: Basic 4   *Round top   [4]
Rows 13   Pointed bottom
* V split at fifth row. String 7 beads in trim color on to each leg of V.

Flower 4: Basic 4   *Round top   [4]
Rows 15   Pointed bottom
* V split at seventh row. String 8 beads in trim color on to each leg of V.

Procedure: Start with a 3″ loop at the top basic, instead of a single top wire. Work for specified number of rows. Untwist the top loop until 2 twists remain under the beads. Split the top basic in half and work as a V split for 8 rows. *Do not cut any wires.* String the required number of beads in the trim color on to each of the V wires and string through to the back of the petal. Twist the 2 wires together at the back. Bend down close to petal and cut away all but ½″.

Centers: 5—¾″ loops, all on one wire, in pale green   [1]

Leaves: Basic 9   Both ends pointed   [10]
Rows 11   ½″ stem shows on all leaves.

Assembly of Flowers:

a. Hold 2 petals face up and 2 petals face down, on top of one another. Twist all stems together as one.

b. Fan out petals.

c. Slide in the center.

d. Tape down stem for 2″.

Assembly of Branch:

a. Tape a #16 stem wire.

b. Tape 1 leaf and 1 small flower to a 6″ piece of #16 stem wire.

c. Stems of leaves extend ½″ away from main branch.

d. Flower stem extends 1″ out from branch.

e. Follow photograph for branch assembly.

Shaping:

This is a very open-faced flower.

Cup each petal in the center, shallowly.

Centers are formed into a circle and then bunched up so that their rounded ends face the sky.

Leaf tips are shallowly bent down.

FABIANA

Materials
#25 gold wire
Violet or white crystal for florets
Dark green for foliage
Brown tape
#16 stem wire

Petals: Horizontal petals
Basic loop 10 beads on right side
Basic loop 8 beads on left side
Rows 7   [21]

Procedure:
Open the basic loop of the petals close to the beads, and use as a single wire. String green beads on to this wire as follows:

Put 2 beads on 3 units; 3, 4, 5, 6, 7 on 2 successive units of each size; 8 beads on the remainder. (These beads become the stem of each petal.)

Foliage: 2–1″ loops, all on one wire [4]
2–1¼″ loops, all on one wire   [4]
2–1½″ loops, all on one wire   [2]

Assembly:
a. Bring sides of petals together to cone shape.

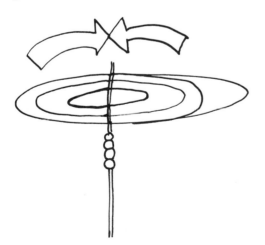

b. Tape a full length of stem wire.
c. Tape one of the 2-bead stems to the top. Pull the bare wire gently down to lock the stem under the tape.

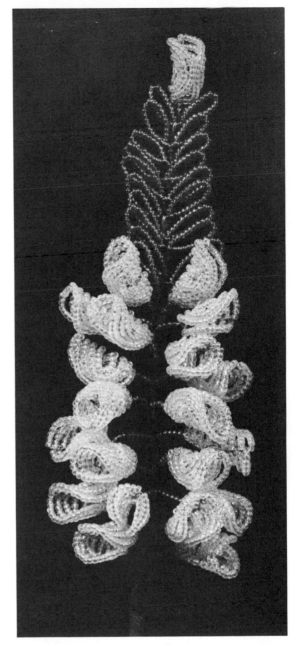

d. Press all loops of the foliage closed. Add them, in the proper order, ½″ under one another, taping them on one at a time.
e. Add the florets, in stem size order, two at a time, ½″ under one another.

Shaping:
All foliage and florets face an east and west position.
Push up gently.

FERNS AND VINES

Materials

#26 and #28 silver wire
Two shades of green
Dark green tape
#18 and #20 stem wire

Fern 1:

a. String on to #28 wire 40″ of dark green, then add a half strand of light.
b. Tape a 12″ piece of #20 stem wire.
c. Anchor the feed wire 5″ up from one end.
d. Make 2–3″ loops on each side of the stem, working around the stem with a full basic turn.
e. Close each loop as you work.
f. Make 2–2⅞″ loops on each side of the stem.

g. Continue to work up the stem in the same manner, making each pair of loops ⅛″ shorter than the previous pair, until a 2″ size is made.
h. A single 2″ loop sits straight up on top. Trim the top of the stem wire just below the top of the single loop. Point all loops toward the top.

Fern 2:

a. String on to #26 wire 2 shades at random. Knot the end of the wire.
b. Leave 2″ of bare wire.
c. Push over 10 beads and make a 3″ loop.
d. Push over 10 beads and make a 2⅞″ loop, close to the 10 beads.
e. Continue in this manner, making each

loop ⅛″ shorter than the previous one. All loops have 10 beads between. Work until a 1″ loop is made.

f. Make 2–1″ loops with no beads between.

g. Repeat all loops, with 10 beads between loops, working backward from the smallest to the largest.

h. Fold the entire unit in half, twist the end wires, and spiral each loop once. Start and finish with 10 beads.

i. Tape a #18 stem wire. Hold the top 1″ loop against the top of the stem and the remainder of the unit running down the stem.

j. Tape the bare wires to the stem wire.

k. Grip the bottom loops and spiral the entire unit around the stem to the top.

CUT-LEAF VINE

Materials

#26 silver wire
Dark and light green
Brown tape
#16 stem wire

Split basic method—5 petals—as follows:

a. Knot the end of the wire.

b. Push over basic count of beads.

c. Allow 3″ of free wire and make 2—4″ basic loops, next to each other.

d. Twist both loops together, where they meet, for ¾″. Place one on top of another.

e. Work the first petal.

f. Open 1 loop, set a wire on each side of the petal, and work the side petals.

g. Open the second loop, set a wire on each side of the unit, and work the bottom petals.

Petal 1:	Basic 5 Rows 11	Pointed top and bottom

Petals 2:	Basic 1″ Rows 5	As above

Petals 3:	Basic 5 Rows 5	As above

Stem: Push over 1″ of beads for a stem. Cut free from spool with 2″ of bare wire.

Leaves: Make 4 leaves in dark green; 4 in light green; 4 shaded by stringing both colors at random.

Assembly:

a. Tape a stem wire, and tape a dark petal to the top, gently pulling down on the bare wire to lock the beaded stem in place, under the tape.

b. Continue to tape the dark leaves 1″ under one another.

c. Add the light and then the shaded leaves, all 1″ under each other.

d. Tape down the entire stem.

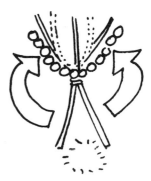

IVY BRANCH

Materials

#26 silver wire
1 each of 3 different shades of green
Dark green tape
#16 and #18 stem wire

Triple split basic on all units.

Unit 1:	Dark green	Basic 11	Pointed top
		Rows 7	and bottom

Split bottom basic and place one petal on each side of first petal in the following count:

		Basic 11	Pointed top
		Rows 5	and bottom

Leave ½" of beads on the feed wire for a stem, and cut free from spool with 2" of bare wire. [8]

Unit 2:	Medium green	Basic 9	As above	
		Rows 7		
	Split petals	Basic 9	As above	
		Rows 5		[6]
Unit 3:	Light green	Basic 7	As above	
		Rows 5		
	Split petals	Basic 7	As above	
		Rows 5		[6]

Assembly:

a. Tape a #16 stem wire and tape a Unit 3 to the top. Pull gently at the bare wire of the leaf to lock the beads of the stem tightly to the main stem.

b. Tape the remainder of Unit 3 all ½" under each other, in the same manner.

c. Add the medium and then the dark leaves, all in the same way.

NOTE: If a denser branch is desired, repeat half of each unit and tape to a #18 stem. Add this to the main branch.

FLAME VIOLET

Materials
#25 gold wire for flower
#26 silver wire for leaves
#32 binding wire
Yellow crystal for centers
Dark orange crystal for flower
Medium green for foliage
Dark green tape
#20 stem wire

Petals:	Basic 6	Round top	
	Rows 7	Pointed bottom	[6]
Centers:	Basic 4	Round top	
	Rows 5	and bottom	[1]
	Last 2 rows are worked in yellow.		
Leaves:	Basic ½″	Pointed top	
	Rows 9	Round bottom	[3]

Assembly of Flower:
a. Place 3 petals face up on top of one another, and 3 face down on top of one another.
b. Twist all hanging wires 3 times close to beads.
c. Fan out petals. Front sides face up.
d. Straddle center across flower.
e. Twist all hanging wires once more.
f. Hook a #20 stem wire through the back of the flower.
g. Close hook.
h. Thin out and shorten hanging wires to 1″.
i. Tape hanging wires to stem for 1¼″.
j. Jewel under flower for 1¼″.
k. Bind bare wire closely under jeweling and cut away.
l. Push stem beads on to stem for 3″.
m. Tape just under stem beads, catching last bead into tape.

Assembly of Leaves:
a. Place all 3 leaves face up on top of one another.

b. Twist hanging stems right under beads 3 times.

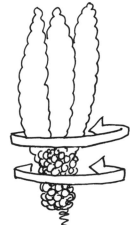

c. Fan leaves out.
d. Hook a #20 stem wire through the center.
e. Work remainder like flower assembly g through k.
f. Push stem beads on to stem for 2″.
g. Attach leaf stem to flower stem, where stem beads end. Bind together with #32 wire.
h. Cut away wire and tape down stem.

Assembly of Spray:
(3 flowers and 9 leaves)
a. Bead flower and leaf stems with varying heights of stem beads.
b. Bind all flowers together with #32 wire.
c. Tape down stem.
d. Bind on one leaf stem at a time, evenly around stem.
e. Tape down stem.

FLOWERING CRAB APPLE BRANCH

Materials

#25 gold and #26 green wire

Multishaded pink and raspberry crystal for flowers

Luster red for foliage

Brown tape

#16 stem wire

Each branch has 6 flowers and 12 leaves.

Centers:	* Single beaded stems, Method	
	II	[6]
#25 gold	Each stem is ¾″ long, in multi-shaded pink.	

Petals:	Raspberry	
#25 gold	Basic 10	Round top	[5]
	Rows 9*	Pointed bottom

* Complete 7 rows; estimate enough wire to make 2 more rows. Cut free from spool and string 3″ of multishaded pink on to the open end of wire. Complete petal.

Leaves:	Luster red on green wire	
	Basic ¾″	Pointed top	[12]
	Rows 9	Round bottom

Assembly:

a. Place 3 petals face up and 2 face down on top of one another.

b. Twist the hanging wires and fan out flat.

c. Insert centers and tape the stem.

d. Tape an 8″ piece of stem wire. Tape 2 leaves to the top.

e. Add a flower 1″ under with ¾″ of stem showing.

f. Add 2 leaves opposite each other 1″ below.

g. Add another flower 1″ below and repeat f. Make 2 stems.

h. Tape a full length of stem wire. Tape a flower to the top.

i. Add 2 leaves 1″ under on opposite sides of the stem.

j. Add one side branch, one flower, two leaves, and a side branch, all 1″ under one another.

k. Tape down the remainder of the stem.

FLOWERING QUINCE

Materials
#26 gold wire for centers
#28 silver wire for flowers
#26 silver wire for foliage
Dark orange chalk for flowers
Dark and medium green
Brown tape
Stem beads
#16 stem wire

Centers:	Medium green
#26 gold	6—¾″ loops, all on one wire, each spiraled into a figure eight [10]
Petals:	5—¾″ 4-row crossovers, with one
#28 silver	wrap, all on one wire [10]
Calyx:	Dark green
#26 silver	5—10-bead loops, all on one wire [10]
Leaves:	String both greens at random.
#26 silver	Basic 9 Pointed top [6]
	Rows 9 and bottom

Assembly of Flower:
a. Insert one center unit into one petal unit. Use one end wire of the center to twist firmly around all hanging wires, tightly against underside of beads. Trim off the end wires of the center unit.
b. Set calyx into position tightly against back of flower, and twist one end wire around the hanging wires, as above. Trim off the end wires of the calyx.
c. String 5 stem beads on to the bare wires of the flower to use as a stem.
d. Twist 2 flowers together to lock the beads in place. Repeat once.
e. Twist 3 flowers together. Repeat once. (You now have all 10 flowers locked into position.)

Assembly of Branch:
a. Tape a 12″ piece of stem wire. Tape 2 leaves to the top.
b. Tape a 2-unit flower assembly ½″ under.
c. Add a 3-unit assembly 1″ under.
d. Tape 2 leaves opposite each other 1″ below.
e. Tape a 2-unit assembly ¾″ below.
f. Add another 3-unit assembly ¾″ below.
g. Tape 2 leaves opposite each other 1″ below.

Shaping:
Cluster all flowers to face front.
Leaves face upward and out.

FRINGED GENTIAN

Materials
#25 gold wire
#32 binding wire
Blue or purple crystal for flower
Yellow crystal for center
Topaz for calyx
Medium green for foliage
Brown tape
#16 stem wire

Center:	4—¾″ loops, all on one wire, in yellow	[1]
Petals:	* Branch method Basic 1″ Round top Rows 3 Pointed bottom Make 1 loop on each side, slightly lower than the top. Make a second loop on each side, slightly lower than the first two.	[4]
Calyx:	4—10-bead loops wrapped once with 3 beads between loops	[1]
Leaves:	Basic 1″ Pointed top Rows 5 and bottom	[2]

Assembly:
a. Tape the top of a 10″ piece of stem wire.
b. Bind on the center and tape the bindings.
c. Add the petals one at a time, overlapping the bottoms.
d. Tape the bindings and add the calyx firmly under the flower.
e. Add the leaves 2″ under the flower on opposite sides of the stem.

Shaping:
Centers are straight up with tips bent out.
The top half of the petals are bent out at right
   angles in a cross shape.

FUCHSIA

Materials

#26 gold wire for centers
#26 silver wire
#32 binding wire
White and red crystal for flowers
Medium green for foliage
Light green tape
#16 and #20 stem wire

Centers:	Red on #26 gold wire.
	Leave 2″ of bare wire. Make a tight 3-bead loop. Leave another 2″ of bare wire. Cut away from spool. Twist and spiral the bare wire for 1½″ under the bead loop. [6]
Petals:	White on #26 silver wire. Split basic *plus* a single petal.
	Basic 7 Pointed top [3 petals
	Rows 5 and bottom total]
Sepals:	Red on #26 silver wire. Split basic.
	Basic 12 Pointed top [2]
	Rows 7 and bottom
Leaves:	Basic 7 Pointed top [6]
	Rows 7 Round bottom
	Basic 9 As above [6]
	Rows 9

Assembly of Flower:

a. Twist the bottoms of 6 center units together for ½″.
b. Tape a 4″ piece of #20 stem wire.
c. Tape the center cluster to the top.
d. Arch the white petals slightly and bind on, spacing evenly around the centers with back side facing in.

e. Tape the bindings.
f. Bind on the red sepals, to fit around, with back sides facing in.
g. Tape the bindings.
h. Tape down and add 2 small leaves 1″ under and opposite each other.
i. Make 3 complete flower stems.

Assembly of Branch:

a. Tape a #16 stem. Bind on and tape a flower branch to the top.
b. Tape 2 large leaves ½″ under, opposite each other.
c. Bind on and tape a flower branch 1″ down.
d. Add 2 large leaves ½″ under.
e. Repeat for the final flower branch.

Shaping:

Curve each flower branch into an arc on one side of the main stem.
White petals are curved up and around the centers.
Red sepals stand straight up around the petals with the tips bent toward the centers.
The large leaves are opposite each other.
The entire branch is curved in an arch over the flowers.

GAILLARDIA

Materials

#26 silver or #24 gold wire for flower (depending on colors used)
#26 silver wire for foliage
#32 binding wire
Any two contrasting colors in chalk or crystal
Dark green for foliage
Dark green tape
#16 stem wire

Petals: Start with Color A on wire.

UNIT 1: 6″ bare wire, then 2″ loop; 2″ crossover; 2″ loop; end with 6″ of bare wire. String 2″ of Color B on the first and last 6″ of bare wire, and complete the single loop as a crossover.   [4]

UNIT 2: 4″ of bare wire. 2–2″crossovers; 1–2″ loop; end with 6″ of bare wire, and complete the single loop as above.   [2]

UNIT 3: 3–2¾″ crossovers   [4]

UNIT 4: 3–3½″ crossovers   [4]

UNIT 5: With color B on wire
3–4¼″ crossovers   [5]

Calyx: 6–3″ crossovers with 2 beads between   [1]

Leaves: * Branch method
Basic 2″   Pointed top   [2]
Rows 3   and bottom
* Add 1–4¾″ crossover on each side. Then add 1–4″ crossover on each side.

Assembly:

a. Twist the hanging wires of one of the first units.
b. Hook on a #16 stem wire. Close hook.

c. Bind on the remaining 3 units of the same size with #32 wire, spacing evenly around stem.
d. Tape bindings for ½″.
e. Bind on the next size, one on each side of the stem.
f. Continue to bind on each size in turn, and tape the bindings.
g. Taper and shorten all hanging wires.
h. Add the calyx just under the flower head, pressing the petals up against the flower.
i. Tape down the entire stem.
j. Add the leaves 3″ below the flower head, 1″ under each other.

GARDENIA

Materials

#26 silver wire
#32 binding wire
White pearl for flower
Dark green for foliage
Dark green tape
#16 and #20 stem wire

Centers:	4—10-bead loops, all on one wire	[1]	
	Cluster together.		
Row 1:	Basic 5	Round top,	[4]
	Rows 7	semipointed bottom	
Row 2:	Basic 5	As above	[6]
	Rows 9		
Row 3:	Basic 7	As above	[8]
	Rows 11		
Calyx:	6—2″ loops with 3 beads between, all on one wire	[1]	
Leaves:	Basic 7	Pointed top	[4]
	Rows 7	and bottom	
	Basic 9	As above	[5]
	Rows 9		
	Tape all leaf stems.		
Bud:	Basic 7	Semipointed top,	1 white,
	Rows 9	round bottom	1 green

Assembly of Bud:

a. Hold the two petals together face up and spiral them around each other.

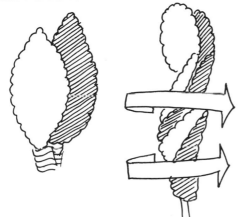

b. Tape to the top of an 8″ piece of #20 stem wire.

c. Tape 2 small leaves 2″ under and opposite each other; ¼″ stem shows.

Assembly of Flower:

a. Twist hanging wires of center loops.
b. Hook a #16 stem through and close hook.
c. Bind on the first row one at a time, spacing evenly around.
d. Tape the bindings for ½″.
e. Bind on each row in turn.
f. Taper and shorten all hanging wires.
g. Tape calyx under the flower. Tape down entire stem.
h. Tape 2 small leaves 1″ under, opposite each other, with ¼″ stem showing.
i. Add a large leaf 1″ below.

Assembly of Branch:

a. Bind on, then tape the bud branch to the flower stem ½″ under the final leaf. Three inches of bud branch shows.
b. Tape 2 large leaves at the joining point, opposite each other.
c. Add 2 large leaves 1″ below, opposite each other.

Shaping:

First row of petals is bent up and out.
Each succeeding row follows this shape, so the top view of the flower is almost flat.
Calyx is pushed tightly against flower.
Bud stem is curved up and out.

GERBERA

Materials

#26 gold wire for centers
#25 gold or #26 silver wire for petals
#26 silver wire for foliage
#32 binding wire
Yellow, orange, or dark pink crystal or cut crystal
Dark and light green for foliage
Dark green tape
Stem beads
#16 and #20 stem wire

Centers: #26 gold		10—1¼″ loops, all on one wire All loops are oval, and set half behind one another.		[5]
Dome Petal:	Light green	Basic 5 Rows 10	Round	[1]
Petals:	Split basic units	Basic 2″ Rows 3	Pointed top and bottom	[12]
Calyx:	Dark green	6—2″ loops, all on one wire		[3]

Leaves:

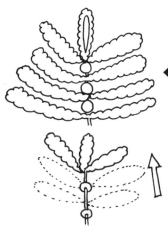

a. Tape the top 1″ of an 8″ piece of #20 stem wire. [2]
b. String #26 silver with dark and light green at random.
c. Slide 16 stem beads on to #20 stem wire and tape the bottom to hold the beads in place.
d. Anchor the feed wire to the top and make 3—1″ loops.
e. One loop sits on top and one goes to each side.
f. Push up 1 stem bead and make a 1″ loop on each side of the stem, tightly against the stem bead.
g. Push up 1 stem bead and make a 1¼″ loop on each side, as above (3 times).
h. Repeat this method with 1½″ loops each side (3 times), then with 1¼″ loops each side (3 times), then with 1″ loops each side (6 times).
i. Tape under the final loop and down the stem.

Assembly:

a. Twist 2 of the center units around the dome petal.

b. Hook a #16 stem wire through and close hook.

c. Bind on the 3 remaining center units to fit around the first 2.

d. Bind on the petal units. Tape the bindings.

e. Twist one end of a calyx unit to another to form a circle. Push up under flower and bind around stem.

f. Taper and shorten all hanging wires and tape down stem.

g. Bind on the leaves one at a time 6″ under the flower, opposite each other.

Shaping:

All petals are curved upward and tips bent out.

Press the calyx firmly up against the flower. The leaves are curved upward and outward.

GLADIOLUS, BABY

Materials

#28 and #26 silver or #25 and #24 gold wire
#34 lacing wire
Any color crystal for flowers
Light green for foliage
Light green tape
Stem beads
#16 and #20 stem wire

Petals:

UNIT 1:	Basic 5 Rows 5	Pointed top and bottom	[15]
UNIT 2:	Basic 7 Rows 7	As above	[10]
UNIT 3:	Basic 7 Rows 9	As above	[36]

Centers:

FOR UNITS 1 AND 2:
2″ of bare wire; 2—10-bead loops; 2″ bare wire [5]
String ¾″ of beads on the 2 hanging wires.

FOR UNIT 3:
As above with 3—10-bead loops [6]

Calyx:

FOR UNITS 1 AND 2:
Basic 7   Pointed top [10]
Rows 5   and bottom

FOR UNIT 3:

        Basic 7   As above   [12]
        Rows 7

Buds: With color make 3 petals of Unit 3 size.
In green make 12 calyx of Unit 3 size.

Leaves: Tape the top 2″ of a #20 stem wire. Push on 9″ of stem beads and tape in place.
Work for 8 more rows in pointed top and round bottom.   [2]
Lace at ⅓ up, ½ up, and ⅓ down from top.

Assembly of Flower:

a. Hold 3 petals of Unit 1, front side up, and 2 petals on top, front side down. Twist hanging wires.
b. Insert a Unit 1 center.
c. Place 2 calyx of Unit 1 just under the flower, one on each side.
d. Twist all hanging wires. Tape stem.
e. Repeat for Unit 2.
f. Repeat for Unit 3, using 6 petals per flower and matching center and calyx for unit.

Assembly of Bud:

a. Hold 2 of the green petals together, front side out, and spiral them together. Make 3.
b. Spiral a single color petal, place a green petal on each side, and spiral over the color petal.
c. Twist all hanging wires. Make 3.

Assembly of Entire Stalk:

a. Tape a #16 stem wire. Tape the green buds to the top ½″ under one another on alternate sides of the stem.
b. Add the color buds just under, ¼″ under each other, as in a.
c. Add Unit 1 flowers with ½″ of stem showing, just under the buds. Flowers are directly under and next to one another, working down the front of the stem.
d. Continue to tape each size in order, in the same manner.
e. Tape down entire stem.
f. Add the 2 leaves at the bottom 3″ of the stalk.

Shaping:

All petals stand straight up with the tips bent back.
The leaves are behind the stem.

GLOBE PHLOX

Materials
#28 silver wire
Yellow, pink, or red crystal for main color
White crystal for contrast
Dark green for foliage
Dark green tape
#16 stem wire

String as follows:

> 2¾″ main color; 12 white beads.
> Five times for each floret.

Floret: 12-bead loop wrapped twice, 5, all
on one wire   [12]

Twist one end wire around the final end wire, tightly under the beads. Trim off, leaving a single hanging wire.

Leaves: Basic 1″   Pointed top   [6]
Rows 5   and bottom

Assembly of Flower:

a. String ¾″ of green on each single hanging stem.
b. Twist 3 together to lock beads in place.

Assembly of Branch:

a. Tape the top 3″ of a 12″ piece of stem wire.

b. Tape a unit of 3 flowers to the top.
c. Add the remaining units just under this to fit evenly around.
d. Add 2 leaves 1″ under the flower, opposite each other.
e. Add the remaining leaves in pairs, opposite each other, ½″ under one another.
f. Tape down the remainder of the stem.

Shaping:
Flowers are shaped into a ball.
Leaves stand straight out with their tips bent
down.

GLOBE THISTLE

Materials
#28 silver wire
#32 binding wire
Blue crystal for flower
Light green for foliage
Light green tape
Stem beads
#16 and #20 stem wire

Petals: 2″ of bare wire, 4–2″ loops,   [20] all on 1 wire; end with 2″ of bare wire. Shape the loops so they stand straight up and the tips bend out in north, south, east, west positions. Twist the bare wires of 5 petals together. Set 1 in the center and 4 all around it in a ball shape. Make 4 sets.

Leaves: [2]
a. Tape 1″ of the top of a #20 stem wire.
b. Tape 2″ of stem beads in position.
c. With feed wire, work 4 rows of pointed top and bottom.
d. Make a 5″ loop on each side, then a 4½″ loop on each side, then a 4″ loop on each side.
e. Continue with the beads on the feed wire and jewel the stem for 1″.
f. Lace halfway up.

Assembly:
a. Tape the top of a #16 stem wire.
b. Bind on 1 set of petals, gently pushing up the loops to form an umbrella shape.
c. Tape the bindings.
d. Add the other 3 sets one at a time, evenly around the first.
e. Tape the bindings.
f. Gently push the loops down to form a ball.
g. Tape down the stem and add a leaf to the back of the stem, and add the second leaf 1″ below on the front of the stem.
h. Tape the remainder of the stem.

Shaping:
The back leaf stands up straight, and the
    front leaf is bent down.

HEATHER

Materials

#26 gold wire
Pink, white, red, or lavender for flower
Medium green for foliage
Brown tape
#16 and #20 stem wire

Unit 1: Leave 2″ of bare wire at the beginning and end of each unit. With color: 17—10-bead loops with 6 beads between loops, all on one wire [8]

Unit 2: With green: Repeat as above [5]

Assembly:

a. Tape the full length of a #16 stem wire.

b. Tape 8–6″ pieces of #20 stem wire.

c. Fold a Unit 1 in half, twist the end wires, draw the sides parallel.

d. Set the top loop over the tip of the #20 stem, and spiral around the stem going down.

e. Tape the hanging wire. (Make 4 stems.)

f. Repeat as above for Unit 2. (Make 3 stems.)

g. Hold a Unit 2 on top of a Unit 1, repeat with stem, and spiral both together, over the stem. (Make 2 stems.)

h. Hold a Unit 1 to the tops of the #16 stem,

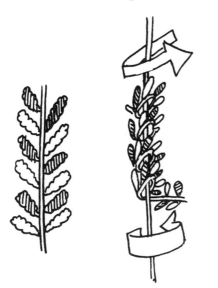

repeat as above, and spiral down the stem.

i. Tape the hanging wire.

j. Hold a Unit 2 on top of a Unit 1, spiral this

just under the white on the #16 stem. Tape the hanging wire, add a white stem just under this, and another white stem, opposite.

k. Add 2 white stems 1″ down, opposite each other, on alternate sides.

l. Add 2 shaded stems 1″ down on opposite sides, alternating sides.

m. Add the 3 green stems 1″ down in a triangular position.

n. Tape down stem.

Shaping:

Bend all stems gently out and up with the tips toward the center branch.

HIBISCUS

Materials

#26 gold wire for centers
#26 silver wire for petals and foliage
Red and yellow for centers
Red crystal for petals
Medium green for foliage
Dark green tape
#16 stem wire

Centers: [5]

Red on gold wire. Leave 3″ of bare wire. Make a single 10-bead loop. Spiral the bare wires for 1″ and cut away from spool, leaving 3″ of bare wire. Twist the bottom 2″ of all 5 centers together.

Yellow on gold wire. Leave 2″ of bare wire. Make 12—10-bead loops with 3 beads between loops, all on one wire. Do *not* cut free from spool.

Hold the bare wire of the yellow running up the 2″ twist of the red. Jewel the twisted bare wire for 1½″. The loops will be just under the 5 single centers and the remainder will be solid yellow.

Petals: Red*   Basic 5   Round top   [5]
          Rows 15   Pointed bottom
* Last 2 rows of each petal may be outlined in yellow if desired.

Calyx: Basic 10   Pointed top   [4]
                Rows 9   Round bottom

Leaves: Basic 12   Pointed top   [3]
                Rows 11   Round bottom

Assembly:

a. Tape the top 2″ of the stem wire.
b. Tape on the center unit.
c. Bind on the petals one at a time and overlap the bottoms.
d. Tape the bindings for ½″.
e. Add the calyx one at a time, spacing evenly around.
f. Thin out and taper the hanging wires.
g. Tape down stem.
h. Add the leaves 2″ under the flower in a triangular position; ½″ of leaf stem shows.
i. Jewel the entire stem for 4″.

Shaping:

The bottoms of the petals overlap and hug the center.

The tips of the petals are bent out at right angles.

The calyx is pressed into the flower with the tips curled back.

INDIGO

Materials

#25 gold wire
Lilac and raspberry crystal for flowers
Light green tape
#16 and #18 stem wire

Flowers: String lilac on spool.
　　　　　Horizontal petal　Basic 8　[24]
　　　　　　　　　　　　　　　Rows 8

a. Cut petal away from spool, leaving 7" of bare wire.
b. Open the bottom basic loop close to the petal.
c. Twist the feed wire and the hanging wire 3 times.
d. String 3" of raspberry on the long wire and 7 raspberry beads on the shorter wire.

e. Make a petal of:
　　　　　Basic 7　Round top
　　　　　Rows 5　Semipointed bottom
f. Cut petal away from spool, leaving 2" of bare wire.
g. Slide 3 green beads on to the bare wire and tape the remaining stem.

Assembly of Flower:

a. Trim top basic wires of both petals.
b. Set raspberry petal over lilac with front sides facing out.
c. Arc the small petal and bring up the sides of the horizontal petal to touch the small petal.

Leaves: Fern type. Each unit makes 1 leaf.
　　　　　Make 6 leaves as follows:

a. String 4" of raspberry on to spool. Make 14 *individual* 10-bead loops with 1" hanging stems. Spiral the hanging stems.
b. String light green on to spool. Leave 8" of bare wire at the beginning.
c. Make 1–10-bead loop. Spiral the 8" piece of wire with the feed wire for 6 full twists.
d. Make 2–10-bead loops, one on each side of the hanging wires.
e. Twist both wires together for 6 full twists.
f. Continue down the stem this way until there are 5 pairs of loops.
g. Add 1 raspberry loop to hanging wires and spiral together for 6 full twists.

h. Make another 5 pairs of green loops and again attach a raspberry.
i. Make 2 more pairs of green loops and cut away from spool, leaving 3" of bare wire. Leaf should have 12 pairs of green loops with 2 raspberry loops.
Make an additional 4 leaves, same method, having 16 pairs of green and 3 raspberry loops.

Assembly of Side Branch:

a. Tape a 6" piece of #18 stem wire.
b. Tape a flower to the top with the beads of stem showing. The raspberry petal faces up.

c. Add 7 more flowers ½" apart, spacing evenly around stem.
d. Add 2 small leaves 1" below on each side of the stem. Repeat for second side branch.

Assembly of Entire Branch:

a. Tape a #16 stem wire.
b. Tape 8 flowers to the stem, just like the side branch.
c. Add the 2 small leaves.
d. Add 1 large leaf 1" below on one side of the stem.
e. Add a side branch on the opposite side of the main stem with 2" of branch stem showing.
f. Add another large leaf ½" below.
g. Add the second branch on the opposite side of the first.
h. Add the 2 remaining large leaves 1" below on opposite sides of the stem.
i. Tape down remainder of stem.

JASMINE

Materials
#28 silver and #26 gold wire
Yellow crystal for florets
Light and dark green for foliage
Light green tape
#16 and #20 stem wire

Florets: Yellow on gold wire
5–1″ loops plus a ½″ loop, all on
one wire   [12]
a. Cut off 3″ of bare wire and string 5 dark
green beads on to this wire. Make a loop of the
green, going around the first hanging wire.
b. Press up into the floret, as a calyx. Trim
away the calyx end wire, close to the bead.
c. String 1″ of dark green on to the first end
wire for a stem.

Buds: Same beads and wire
2–½″loops, all on one wire   [16]
a. Cut off 2″ of bare wire. Twist one end
wire around the other, tightly against the
beads.
b. Trim off one wire. String 4 dark green
beads on to hanging wire for a stem.

Leaves: Dark green on the silver wire; add
7 light green for each leaf.
Basic 7   Pointed top   [23]
Rows 7*   and bottom
* After completing fifth row, estimate enough wire to complete petal
and cut away from spool. String on
light green and finish petal.

Assembly of Florets:

a. Set the small loop into the center and the
5 loops evenly around.
b. All loops stand straight up, the tips of the
outer 5 are bent back.
c. Twist the bare wires of 3 together, as a
unit.

Assembly of Buds:

a. Set the 2 loops together, side by side.
b. Twist the bare wires of 4 together, as a
unit.

Assembly of Leaves:

a. Tape 4–6″ pieces of #20 stem wire.
b. Tape one leaf to the top, add 2 more ½″
under, opposite one another.
c. Add 2 more ½″ under, in the same manner. Make 4 branches.

Assembly of Main Branch:

a. Tape a full length of #16 stem wire.
b. Tape 1 leaf to the top and two ½″ under,
opposite each other.
c. Add a leaf stem 1″ under on one side.
d. Twist the bare wires of a flower and bud
unit together. Add this to the connecting point
of the leaf stem and main branch.
e. Add a leaf stem 1″ under on the opposite
side.
f. Add a flower and bud unit as above.
g. Continue to add a leaf stem and a flower
unit, all in the same manner.
h. Tape down entire stem.

LILY, ATAMASCO

Materials

#28 silver, #28 gold, and #25 gold wire
Any two shades of a color in crystal
Light green for foliage
Light green tape
Stem beads
#16 stem wire

Leave 6″ of free wire at the beginning and end of all petals.

Color 1: 6—2¼″ 4-row crossovers, all on
#28 silver one wire

Color 2: 6—2¼″ 4-row crossovers, all on
#28 silver one wire
String as follows for a two-color flower, same size as above: 4″ dark, 6″ light, 6″ dark, 6″ light, 6″ dark.

Centers: a. Start with 3″ of green on the
#28 gold wire. For each center add ¾″ of dark color.

b. String the wire back into 1″ of the green beads, leaving the dark beads for a loop. Flatten the loop.
c. Twist the hanging wires of all 3 together to form 1 unit.   [3]
Calyx: 6—1″ loops, all on one wire   [3]
#25 gold

Leaves: 3—6″ 4-row crossovers, all on one
#25 gold wire   [1]
3—8″ 4-row crossovers, all on one wire   [1]
Spiral all petals.

Assembly:
a. hold the petals of one flower in a circle.
b. Set in a center unit. Twist the end wires of the center only, twice around the wires of the flower.

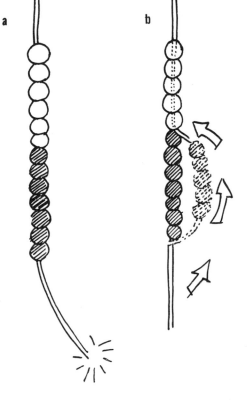

c. Cut off the end wires of the center, close to the flower. (No extra wire is to hang down the stem.)

d. Set one calyx tightly under the flower and use one wire to secure it to the flower with only two turns, and cut off close to stem.

e. String stem beads on the 3 free wires of the stem. Two flowers have 2″ of stem beads, one has 3″ of stem beads.

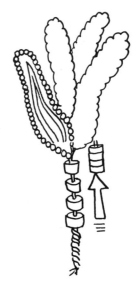

f. Tape the wire under the stem beads to lock them firmly in place.

g. Twist the three stems of the flowers together and tape to a short piece of #16 stem wire.

h. Set the unit of small leaves just under the flower and tape to stem.

i. Set the unit of larger leaves just under this and tape to stem.

Shaping:

Flower petals are curved upward with the tips bent back.

Leaves are shaped the same way.

LILY, CALLA

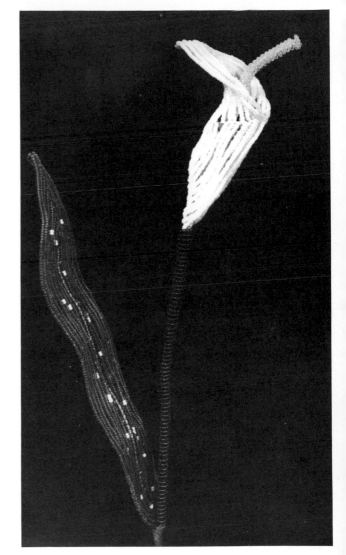

Materials

#25 and #28 gold wire
#26 green wire for foliage
#32 binding wire
White and yellow for centers
Alabaster white, pink, yellow, or white pearl
Dark green for foliage
Yellow and dark green tape
Stem beads
#16 and #20 stem wire

Stamen: Yellow. Tape the top 3″ of a full
#28 gold   length of #16 wire with yellow
tape. Do the remainder with dark
green tape. Jewel the top 3″.

Petal:

a.   Cut 2–6″ pieces of #25 gold wire, and hold aside to be used for an additional basic wire.
b.   Start with 4 double strands of color on #25 gold wire.
c.   Horizontal petal: 4″ of wire for a top basic.
       6″ loop for a bottom basic.
d.   Make a 1″ loop on the right side and go around the top basic as a horizontal petal. Make a 2″ loop on the left side and go around the bottom basic.

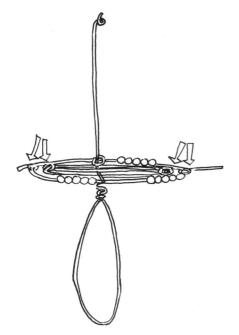

e.   Work the second round over both loops.
f.   With the back side facing up, secure one of the 6″ pieces of #25 gold wire to the first long loop made. Lace it around the second long loop and set it straight out. This becomes another basic wire to work around.
g.   With the front side up, do the same to the first short loop made. You will now have 4 basic wires in a cross position. *The long loop is the top of the petal. Use the reverse basic method on this end only.*
h.   Start to work around each basic wire in a semipoint and graduate to a full point. Work for 29 rows, counting each line of beads at the short end loop.

Leaves:

a. String 3 double strands of green on the green wire, picking up 3 white beads at random places every 2 to 4 inches.

b. Tape the top 4″ of a **#20** stem wire with green floral tape.

c. String 6″ of stem beads and tape them in place.

d. Tape down the stem.

e. Work the feed wire for 14 more rows, pointed top and round bottom. Lace at ⅓ down and ⅓ up.   [2]

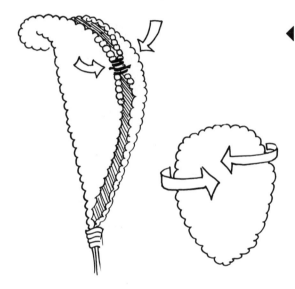

Assembly:

a. Cone-shape the petal by bringing the two side points together, front side out.

b. Twist the end wires and set them to the inside, after you trim them.

c. Bend the top back at a right angle and shape the bottom into a cone.

d. Set the stamen stem down into the flower. Allow 1″ to show above the bend of the petal.

e. Secure this to the first loop made with a short piece of **#28** gold wire.

f. Tape the hanging wire and tape down with green floral tape.

g. Tape the leaf to the flower stem with 2″ of leaf showing above the flower.

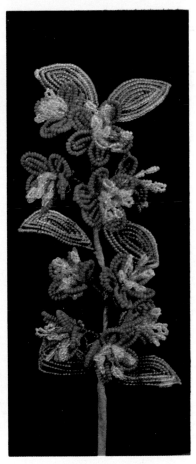

Flame Violet, Veronica, and Cup of Gold

Flowering Quince

Blue Lace, Begonia, and Globe Phlox

Picture Frame

Peppermint Zinnia

Camellia and Saucer Magnolia

Clematis

Mutisia

LILY, KAFFIR

Materials

#28 gold wire for centers
#25 gold wire for petals
#26 silver wire for foliage
#32 binding wire
#34 lacing wire
Yellow and orange crystal for flower
Dark and light green for foliage
Light green tape
Stem beads
#16 and #20 stem wire

Centers: * Single beaded stems,
Method I   [30]
With yellow on #28 gold, add 1 orange bead for each stamen. ¾" yellow, cut away 2" of bare wire. String the first end wire over the orange bead and back through the yellow. Twist 3 together to have 10 units.

Petals: String ⅝" yellow, 1⅞" orange,
PART 1: 1" yellow, ⅞" orange, ¾" yellow, ⅝" orange, ⅝" yellow.
Basic 7   Round top   [30]
Rows 7   Pointed bottom
PART 2: Orange only
Basic 7   As above   [30]
Rows 7

Leaves: * Advanced procedures, using stem bead as a basic. All leaves have pointed tops and round bottoms.
UNIT 1: Dark green. String 6" of stem beads on a 12" piece of #20 stem wire. Work for 8 rows. Lace across center.   [1]
UNIT 2: String 5" of stem beads. Work for 6 rows.   [1]
UNIT 3: Light green. 4" of stem beads. Work for 6 rows.   [1]
UNIT 4: Light green. 3" of stem beads. Work for 6 rows.   [2]

Assembly:

a. Hold 2 petals of Part 1 together, face to face, and twist hanging wires. Set them side by side, add a third petal in a triangular position, face to face, and twist hanging wires.
b. Insert a center unit. Twist hanging wires. Petals are faced up with tips bent back.
c. Tape stems.
d. Tape 3 petals of Part 2 one at a time to fit around this, between center petals. All are face in, straight up, and tips bent back.
e. Tape down stem for 3". (This is one floret.) Make 10 florets. Twist 5 stems together at the bottoms for 1½", to have 2 clusters.

f. Tape a #16 stem wire. Bind on the 2 clusters to the top, one on each side, and tape the bindings.

g. Tape down entire stem.

h. With light green, jewel the stem for 6″.

i. Hold leaf Unit 1 on the back of leaf Unit 2, both facing front, and tape to the back side of the stem, just under the jeweling.

j. Hold one of leaf Unit 4 on the back of the other. Place leaf Unit 3 at the back of this, all facing front, and tape to the front of the stem.

Shaping:

Florets are shaped like an umbrella.

Tip of each leaf is bent toward flower.

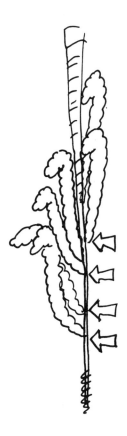

LILY, RED BAND

Materials

#25 gold wire for centers
#26 silver wire for flower
#32 binding wire
#34 lacing wire
White and red speckled chalk beads, plus red chalk
Dark and light green crystal
Light green tape
#16 stem wire

Centers: String 8″ of light green for each stamen. Add 1¼″ of red. Form the red beads into a loop, twisting securely just under the loop. Cut starting wire away from loop and push 1½″ of green close to loop. Cut free from spool, leaving 2″ of bare wire. [6]

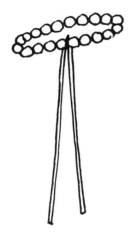

Petals: Speckled bead.
For each petal, add 6″ of solid red beads.
* Reverse basic method

Basic 1¾″	Elongated top	[3]
Rows 7*	and bottom	
Basic 1¾″	As above	[3]
Rows 9*		

Leaves: Light green

Basic 3″	Pointed top	[6]
Rows 5	and bottom	
Lace across center.		

Assembly:

a. Twist hanging wires of all 6 centers together.

b. Hook a #16 stem wire through. Close hook.

c. Tape for ¾″.

d. Bind on the first 3 petals to fit evenly around stem.

e. Tape bindings for ½″.

f. Bind on the next 3 petals to fit between the openings of the first 3.

g. Tape the bindings for ½″.

h. Taper and shorten all hanging wires.

i. Tape down entire stem.

j. With dark green on the #32 wire, jewel down the stem for 5″.

k. Tape 3 leaves at the base of the jeweling, spacing evenly around stem.

l. Add the remaining 3 just under.

m. Tape down stem.

Shaping:

Bend the tips of the outer petals very sharply downward.

Bend the tips of the inner petals down a little more shallowly.

Outer leaves are bent like outer petals.

Inner leaves are bent like inner petals.

LUPINE

Materials
#28 and #26 silver wire
#32 binding wire
Pink, blue, red, purple, or turquoise crystal
Medium green for foliage
Light green tape
#16 stem wire

Use #28 for the following units:

Unit 1: 1–1″ 4-row crossovers, all on one
wire   [1]

Unit 2: 5–¾″ 4-row crossovers, all on one
wire   [1]

Unit 3: 5–1″ 4-row crossovers, all on one
wire   [1]

Unit 4: 6–1¼″ 4-row crossovers, all on one
wire   [1]

Unit 5: 6–1½″ 4-row crossovers, all on one
wire   [1]
Leave at least ⅛″ of wire between
petals.

The rest of the flower is worked on #26.

Unit 6: Basic ½″   Round top   [4]
Rows 5   Pointed bottom

Unit 7: *Basic ½″   Round top   [4]
Rows 5   Pointed bottom
*Split basic

Unit 8: Horizontal petals   [4]
* Set the single petal on top of the
oval petal. Bend edges of oval toward each other, encasing the single
petal.

Basic 10
Rows 6
Cut the basic loop in half and use 1 leg.

Basic 10   Round top
Rows 5   Pointed bottom

Unit 9:   Horizontal petals   [16]
Basic 12
Rows 10
Cut the basic loop in half and use both legs.

Basic 12   Round top
Rows 5   Pointed bottom

Shape the 2 upright petals as a tent. Bend oval petals around to encompass tent petals.

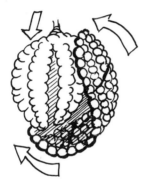

Leaves: Basic ¾″   Both ends   [3]
Rows 7   pointed
Basic 1″   [3]
Rows 5   As above
Basic 1½″   [3]
Rows 7   As above
Basic 5   Very round   [1]
Rows 6   top and bottom

Assembly:

a. Tape a #16 stem wire.

b. Tape the first petal to the top.

c. Add the next sizes all around the stem, about ½″ under one another. (Each size is 1 separate row.) Divide Unit 9 into 3 rows of 4-6-6 petals.

d. When the *single* petal unit is added to stem, start adding the successive units ¾″ under one another.

e. Leaves are assembled with each size next to the other in a circle. The longest leaves face the front. Twist all hanging wires.

f. After all leaves are attached, slide the round center across the top.

g. Each leaf is bound and taped to its own piece of #16 stem wire.

h. Join the leaf stem to the main stem with #32 wire, 3″ under the flower, with one leaf on each side of the main stem.

i. Tape down remainder of stems.

LYTHRUM

Materials

#28 silver wire
Pink, red, apricot, peach, or purple crystal for flower
Dark green for foliage
Dark green tape
#16 stem wire

Buds: Start with green on wire, then add 1¾″ of color for each bud.
4–1¾″ loops, all on one wire [10]

Florets: Leave 2″ of bare wire at start of each floret.
6–2″ loops, all on one wire, ending with 2″ of bare wire [20]

Leaves: Basic 1″   Pointed top   [4]
Rows 9   and bottom

Assembly of Buds:

a. Spiral the color loop. Set the green around in a triangle.
b. Stand the loops straight up with the green tips bent back.

Assembly of Florets:

a. String ¾″ of green on each hanging leg. Twist the end wires.
b. Spiral the green stems. Angle all loops into a cone shape.

Assembly of Branch:

a. Tape a #16 stem wire for full length.
b. Tape a bud to the top. Pull down gently on the bare wire to lock it tightly to the stem.
c. Add the remainder of the buds ½″ under one another evenly around.
d. Add the florets in the same manner, taping on one at a time.
e. Add 2 leaves 1″ under the final row, opposite each other.
f. Add 2 more leaves 1″ under in the opposite direction.
g. Tape down remainder of stem.

Shaping:

All buds and florets are angled away from stem and point upward.
Leaf tips are curled downward.

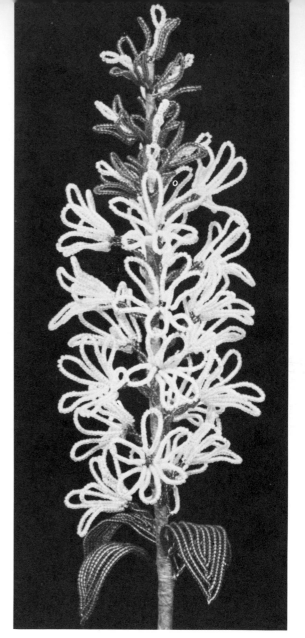

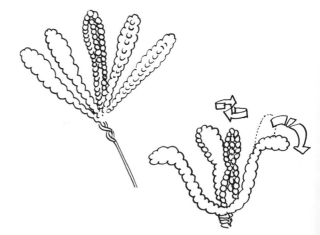

MAGNOLIA, SAUCER

Materials

#26 silver wire
#32 binding wire
White and raspberry crystal for petals
Topaz for jeweling and calyx
Medium green for foliage
Brown tape
#16 stem wire

Inner Petals: White

Basic 3 Round top [3]
Rows 15 Pointed bottom
After seventh row, reduce each row by 1 bead.

Outer Petals: String as follows for each petal, reading across:

Raspberry	White	Raspberry	White	Raspberry	White
1¾″	2¾″	3¼″	2½″	3″	2″
3¼″	1½″	2½″	1½″	2¼″	1¼″
2″	¾″	1¼″	¾″	⅞″	½″
2 beads	5 beads				

Basic 5 Round top [4]
Rows 19 Pointed bottom
After ninth row, reduce each row by 1 bead.

Bud: Raspberry

Basic 3 Round top [3]
Rows 11 Pointed bottom

Calyx:

Basic 5 Round top [9]
Rows 5 Semipointed bottom

Leaves:

Basic 7 Round top [4]
Rows 11 Semipointed bottom
Basic 9 As above [4]
Rows 15

Each branch should have 2 flowers and 2 buds. The count given in the design is for 1 flower and 1 bud.

Assembly:

a. Twist all hanging wires of center petals securely.

b. Hook on a #16 stem wire. Close hook.

c. Tape for ¾". (Make sure the 3 petals have the front sides facing out and standing straight up.)

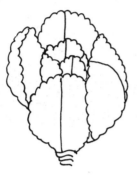

d. Bind on the outer petals one at a time, spacing evenly around. (Face them like the inner petals.)

e. Taper and shorten hanging wires.

f. Tape down entire stem.

g. Bind on 5 calyxes and tape bindings. Wrong sides of calyxes hug flower.

h. Jewel down the stem for 1". Do not cut away the jeweling wire.

i. Tape one small leaf on each side of the stem and jewel over them for 1".

j. Tape one large leaf on each side of the stem and jewel over them for 1½".

Assembly of Bud Stem:

a. Tape the 3 petals to a #16 stem wire about 6" long.

b. Bind on 4 calyxes, evenly around stem, hugging the bud.

c. Cut away binding wire, taper hanging wires, and tape down stem.

d. Add a small leaf on each side of the stem 1" below bud.

e. Tape on the 2 larger leaves 1" below these.

f. Jewel bud stem below calyx, all the way down to 1" below the final leaves.

g. Bind bud stem to flower stem and jewel together for 2½".

MAGNOLIA, SOUTHERN

Materials
#25 gold wire for centers
#26 silver or #26 white enameled wire
#26 silver wire for foliage
#32 binding wire
Topaz and wheat crystal for centers
White chalk for petals
Dark green and white alabaster for foliage
Dark green tape
#16 stem wire

Centers:

UNIT 1:	Wheat	Six 1½″ loops, all on one wire		[2]
UNIT 2:	Topaz	Basic 4	Dome petal	[1]
		Rows 16		

UNIT 3: String 2 colors as follows: Start with ½″ topaz; 1″ wheat; 1″ topaz; 1″ wheat; until there are 7 sections of wheat; then end with ½″ of topaz.

		7–2″ loops, all on one wire	[2]

Bud:

UNIT 1:	Lantern assembly*	Basic 7	Pointed top	[4]
		Rows 7	and bottom	
UNIT 2:	*Reverse basic	Basic 5	Round top*	[4]
		Rows 11	Semipointed bottom	

After seventh row, reduce petal by 1 bead on each row. Force top into a cup shape, keep pointed end flat.

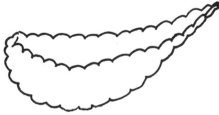

Flower:

UNIT 1: *Reverse basic on all units.

	Basic 7	Round top*	[4]
	Rows 13	Semipointed bottom	

After ninth row, reduce by 1 bead on each row. Force top into a cup shape, keep pointed end flat.

UNIT 2:	Basic 9	As above	[5]
	Rows 15		

Follow instructions for Unit 1. Reduce after eleventh row.

| UNIT 3: | Basic 9 | Round top | [4] |
| | Rows 19 | Semipointed bottom | |

Work as Unit 1. Reduce after the thirteenth row.

Leaves:	Random coloring. For every 5″ green, add 1″ white alabaster.
Bud Leaves:	Basic ¾″	Pointed top	[7]
	Rows 9	and bottom*	

*Bind feed wire very tightly against the beads. *Do not cut away.* Push over ½″ of beads and use this as a stem. Cut away from spool, leaving 2″ of bare wire. Tape under beads. Cut away all but ¼″ of bottom basic loop and press to back of leaf.

| Flower Leaves: | Basic 1″ | | [8] |
| | Rows 9 | As above | |

Assembly of Bud:

a. Assemble Unit 1 as a lantern.
b. Tape a 6″ piece of stem wire.
c. Tape lantern assembly to top.
d. Bind on petals of Unit 2, spacing evenly around.
e. Taper and shorten hanging wires.
f. Tape down stem.
g. Tape 4 leaves ½″ under the bud, close to the stem, evenly around.
h. Tape on the final 3 leaves in a triangular position, ½″ below.

Assembly of Flower Stem:

a. Twist hanging wires of dome petal securely under back.
b. Hook a #16 stem through wires. Close hook.
c. Tape dome to stem for ¾″.
d. With #32 wire, bind on both parts of Unit 1 to stem.
e. Bind on Unit 3 in the same manner.
f. Tape for ¾″.
g. Bind on petals of each unit, spacing evenly around stem, with one unit just under another.
h. Taper and shorten hanging wires and tape down stem.

i. Tape 6 leaves evenly around stem, 1″ under the flower.
j. Add 2 more 2″ below, opposite one another.
k. Bind bud branch to flower stem, 1″ below the last leaves.
l. Tape remainder of stem.

Shaping:

Bud petals point up at an angle, around the center.
Petals curve in.
4 leaves are pressed up around the flower with the tips bent back.
The lower 3 leaves stand out straight.

Flower Shaping:

Center loops all curve around dome.
The first row of petals angles up, touching the loops, with the tops curved inward.
The second row angles up.
The outer row stands straight out.
6 leaves are pressed up around the flower with the tips bent back.
The lower 2 leaves stand out straight.

MARIGOLD, NAUGHTY MARIETTA

Materials

#25 gold wire
#32 binding wire
Yellow chalk or crystal
Brown crystal
Dark green for foliage
Dark green tape
#16 stem wire

Centers:			
UNIT 1:	Yellow	3—1″ 4-row crossovers, all on one wire	[1]
UNIT 2:	Brown	6—1½″ loops, all on one wire	[1]
		7—1¾″ loops, all on one wire	[1]
Petals:	Yellow	Basic 7 Round top	[7]
		Rows 9 Pointed bottom	

Leaves:
a. Fold 4″ of bare wire in half and tape it.
b. Make a 1½″ loop on top of this base.
c. Make a 1½″ loop on each side, using the taped wire as a basic.
d. Make 2 more 1½″ loops on each side.
e. Make a 1¾″ loop on each side.
f. Tape the final end wire to the basic.   [2]

Assembly:

a. Set the 3 center units around one another, from small to large.
b. Twist all hanging wires.
c. Hook the stem wire on and close the hook.
d. Bind on the petals one at a time, overlapping the bottoms.
e. Taper and shorten the hanging wires. Tape down the stem.
f. Add 1 leaf 2″ under the flower with ½″ of stem showing.
g. Add the second leaf ½″ below.
h. Tape down stem.

Shaping:

Yellow center stands upright with first row of brown nestled around it.
Petals stand out horizontally, and long brown loops are pressed down onto them, in a circle.

MOSS ROSE

Materials
#28 silver wire
Any color crystal for flowers
Medium green for foliage
Light green tape
#18 stem wire

Petals:
UNIT 1: 3—9-bead loops wrapped once, all on one wire [2]

UNIT 2: 7—12-bead loops wrapped twice, all on one wire [1]

Bud:
4—9-bead loops wrapped once, all on one wire [1]

Calyx:
4—9-bead loops with a loose wrap, 3 beads between loops, ending with 3 beads [1]

Leaves:
Leave 3″ of bare wire at beginning and end of petal. A single 10-bead loop with 2 loose wraps [4]

Assembly:
a. Shape the petals of Unit 1 as a hairpin. Set one within another. Twist hanging wires.
b. Tape a 4″ piece of stem wire.
c. Tape Unit 1 to stem wire.
d. Tape Unit 2 directly under to fit evenly around.
e. Point the outer loop of the calyx and tape directly under flower.
f. Tape down stem.
g. Tape the leaf stems, then twist the bottom 1″ of three together.
h. Tape to the flower 2″ under flower head.
i. Nest the bud on the final leaf and tape the stem for 2″.
j. Tape to flower stem, opposite the 3 leaves.

Shaping:
Gently press all petals of flower into a ball shape.
Press calyx against petals.
Fan out leaf stems, side by side, in a slight arc shape.

MOUNTAIN LAUREL

Materials

#26 and #25 gold wire for flowers
#26 green wire for foliage
#32 binding wire
Multishaded pink and raspberry crystal for flowers
Dark and medium green for foliage
Brown tape
#16 stem wire

Flowers: #25 gold	Multishaded pink	Basic 4 Rows 11	Round top and bottom	[15]

Work very tightly to cone-shape. Cut away both basics and press against petal.

Centers: #26 gold	Raspberry	*Single beaded stems, Method II Make 8 bead stems. Work them in pairs.	[75 pairs]

Buds: #26 gold	Raspberry	3—1¼″ 3-row crossovers, all on one wire [8]

Leaves:	String dark green on green wire, picking up 1″ of light green at random.

Basic 1″ Rows 7	Pointed top and bottom	[3]
Basic 1½″ Rows 7	As above	[6]

Assembly of Flowers:

a. Twist 2 pairs of centers together, for 15 units. Twist 3 pairs of centers together, for 15 units.

b. Pinch the upper edge of the flower cone at 5 places, to star shape.

c. Set 1 double unit of center through the cone, on one side of the basic row.

d. Set 1 triple unit of center through the other side of the basic row.

e. Twist the hanging wires. Tape the bare-wire stem.

Assembly of Buds:

With bare wire on the inside, shape as a lantern, tape the stem.

Assembly of Branch:

a. Tape the leaf stems. Twist 2 large and 1 small as a unit.

b. Tape a #16 stem wire.

c. Tape 1 unit of leaves to the top with ½″ of stem showing.

d. Bind on 1 flower 1″ under with 1″ of stem showing.

e. Bind on 4 more flowers, just next to and just under, the first (forming a cluster).

f. Set this cluster to one side of the stem.

g. Tape the bindings.

h. Bind on 5 flowers plus 4 buds in the same way, at a triangular corner to the first cluster. The buds are on the underside.

i. Bind on the final 5 flowers plus 4 buds to form the third part of the triangle.

j. Tape all bindings.

k. Tape a leaf unit 2″ under the flower. The final leaf unit goes 1″ under.

l. Tape down the stem.

Shaping:

All flowers are clustered around the top of the stem.

All leaves stand straight out and fan out.

MUTISIA

Materials

#25 gold and #26 silver wire.
#26 green wire
Topaz and brown crystal for centers
Any light color for flowers, in crystal
Dark and medium green for foliage
Brown tape
Stem beads
#16 stem wire

Flowers: 6–2″ 4-row crossovers, all on one wire [1]
8–2″ 4-row crossovers, all on one wire [2]

Centers: Topaz on gold wire [1]
Make 6–1″ loops. Narrow the loops. Cut away 10″ of feed wire. On to this, string 7½″ of brown and make 6–1¼″ loops. Narrow the loops. Set the dark loops around the topaz. Using 1 leg only, twist tightly under the beads and cut away.

Calyx:	Dark green on green wire 1″ loop wrapped once, with 2 beads between loops, 5, all on one wire [1]
Bud:	6–2″ loops, all on one wire [1] Narrow the loops.
Bud Calyx:	Dark green on green wire 3–12-bead loops, wrapped once, all on one wire, with 2 beads between each set of loops [1]
Leaves:	Dark green on green wire Leave 8″ of free wire on top basic. Basic 1″ Both ends [5] Rows 11* pointed

a. *On fourth row, push down 6 beads, make a 3″ horizontal loop of bare wire. Keep this close to the 6 beads. Repeat this 2 more times. Work the basic turn, and then push down as many beads needed to match the first side.

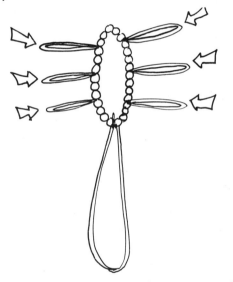

b. Continue around, using the loops as a basic turn. Make a point each time by adding 1 extra bead to form a U-shape.
c. Continue around until 11 rows are completed.
d. String 6″ of light green on the top basic.
e. Push down tightly against leaf and make a 10-bead loop at the top.

f. Cut end wire close to the beads.
g. Spiral this around a pencil.

h. Cut all protruding wire and bend back as a basic.

Assembly:
a. Set bud into bud calyx. Use 1 leg of calyx to twist around bud stem. Cut away. Add 1″ of stem beads.
b. Tape hanging wires.
c. Tape a #16 stem wire and tape the bud to the top.
d. Set the center into the flower. Set the flower into the calyx.
e. Use 1 leg of the calyx to twist around under the flower. Cut away.
f. String on 1″ of stem beads.
g. Tape under the stem beads.
h. Tape 1 leaf 1″ under the bud.
i. Add a small flower, then 1 leaf.
j. Add 1 larger flower with 2 leaves opposite each other.
k. Add another large flower with the last leaf.

NIGHT-BLOOMING CEREUS

Materials

#25 gold wire for flower
#26 green wire for foliage
Any color crystal for flower, with a contrast for the center
Dark green for foliage
Dark green tape
#16 and #18 stem wire

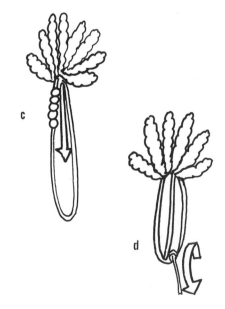

Petals:	Basic 1¼″	Pointed top	[6]
	Rows 9	Round bottom	
	Basic 1¾″	As above	[6]
	Rows 9		

Center 1: 10–1¼″ loops, all on one wire [1]

  a. Connect into a circle and spiral all loops.

  b. Measure 4″ of beads under this and form into a loop.

  c. Push over enough beads to reach the bottom of the loop.

  d. Cut off 4″ of bare wire and secure through bottom of loop. Spiral all three rows of beads.

e. Twist top wire under the head and cut away.

Center 2: *Single beaded stems, Method II Stems are 1¾″ long. Make in units of 3 pairs. (Make 7 units of 6 individual stems.)   [42 single]

Calyx: 6—6″ 4-row crossovers, all on one wire   [2]

Leave about ½″ bare wire between loops. Make each unit in a different color. Topaz and brown are recommended.

Leaves: 14″ of #18 stem wire taped in green   [2]

a. Anchor the feed wire 6″ up from the bottom of the stem.

b. Cover the exposed wire with tape.

c. The basic count rests against the stem wire, which is used as a top and bottom basic.

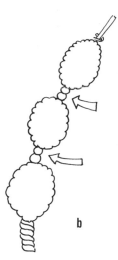

b

Make 7 petals as follows:

Basic 6   Round top
Rows 9   and bottom

d. When completing each petal, twist the bare wire up the stem for ½″. This permits enough room to complete the next petal.

e. When the last petal is completed, wind the feed wire around the tip of the stem.

f. Cover the exposed wire with tape and cut away all but ½″ of stem. This ½″ stands up straight.

Assembly:

a. Twist all hanging wires of Center 2 together.

b. Set Center 1 in the middle.

c. Hook a #16 stem through the wires. Close hook.

d. Tape for 1″.

e. Bind on all petals of small size one at a time, spacing evenly around.

f. Tape bindings for ½″.

g. Bind on all petals of the larger size, just under the smaller ones.

h. Thin out and taper the hanging wires and tape for 1″.

i. Add each row of the calyx by binding on with #32 wire.

j. Tape down entire stem.

k. Add one leaf stem on each side of the flower about 3″ below the flower head. Bind on with #32 and then tape down entire stem.

Shaping:

Center 1 stands straight up.
Centers 2 are fluffed all around 1.
First row of petals curls toward center.
Second row stands up straight.
Calyx has one color bent up toward flower and second color bent down toward stem.
Leaves gently arc away from the main stem.

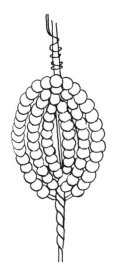

ORANGE BLOSSOMS

Materials

#28 silver wire for flowers
#26 silver wire for foliage
White pearl for blossoms, yellow crystal for centers
Dark green for foliage
Dark green tape
#16 stem wire

Spray consists of 1 bud, 2–3-petal buds, 1 half-open bud, 2 full flowers, 2 small leaves, 2 large leaves.

Leave 3″ stems at beginning and end of all parts.

Full Flower:	5–1⅝″ 4-row crossovers, all on one wire	[2]
CENTER:	4–½″ stems, coil ends	[2]
CALYX:	4–1″ loops wrapped once, all on one wire	[2]
Half-open Bud:	4 petals like full flower	[1]
CENTER:	2–½″ stems, coil ends	[1]
CALYX:	4–1¼″ loops, all on one wire	[1]
3-petal Bud:	3–1½″ 4-row crossovers, all on one wire	[2]
CALYX:	3–1¼″ loops, all on one wire	[2]
Bud:	3–1″ 4-row crossovers, all on one wire	[1]
CALYX:	3–1″ loops, all on one wire	[1]
Leaves:	Basic 7 Pointed top Rows 9 Round bottom	[2]
	Basic 9 As above Rows 11	[2]

Assembly of Flowers and Buds:

a. Place stamen in center of flower and twist all wires together just under flower.
b. Place calyx against back of flower and twist all wires once again.
c. Tape hanging wires.

Assembly of Spray:

a. Tape a #16 stem wire.
b. Tape each section on individually in the following manner:

Tape a bud to the top with 1½″ of bud stem extending beyond the top of the stem wire.
Tape 1 small leaf to the top of stem wire with ½″ of leaf stem extending away from main stem.
Tape a full flower 1″ below with 1½″ of flower stem showing beyond stem wire.
Tape a second small leaf next to the flower with ½″ of leaf stem exposed.
c. Continue down stem as in diagram.

ORCHID CORSAGE

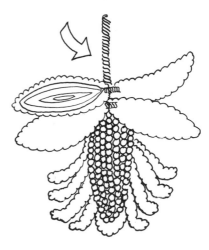

Materials

#25 gold wire
#32 gold lacing wire
Yellow crystal for center
Two shades of purple or purple and white crystal
A 5 x 10 piece of nylon net for the bow
White tape

Unit 1: Start with one strand of light on the wire and add 15″ of dark.

> Basic ¾″   Round top
> Rows 11   Pointed bottom

Continue on the same wire and make 2—4″ loops on each side, then 2—3¾″ loops on each side. Lace half-way up.   [1]

Unit 2: Light shade only

> Basic ¾″   Semipointed top
> Rows 11   and bottom   [2]

Unit 3: Light shade only   *Split basic

> Basic 1″   Semipointed top
> Rows 7   and bottom

Make a single petal of the same size.   [3 in all]

Center: Basic 5   Round top

> Rows 5   and bottom

Continue on the same wire and make a 1½″ loop. Spiral the loop and rest it on the round petal.   [1]

side of the single petal. (Large petal should be face up with 5 petals face down.) Gently turn the 5 petals back, to show face up.

Assembly:

a. With center unit on the large petal, front sides up, twist the hanging wires.

b. Hold petal of Unit 2, face to face, on one side of Unit 1. Twist hanging wires. Repeat with second petal of Unit 2, on opposite side.

c. Hold the single petal of Unit 3 face down over the midpoint of the 2 side petals. Twist the bare wire and the 2-petal unit on each

d. The base of all petals should meet. Bring up the side loops and bend tips down.

e. Gather the nylon together, down the 10″ side, using a 6″ piece of lacing wire to hold it together. Fan out the sides and place the bow just under the flower. Twist the wires.

f. Tape the wire and use a corsage pin to secure to garment.

PASSIONFLOWER

Materials

#26 and #28 silver wire for flower and foliage

#32 binding wire

White and a small amount of blue or violet crystal for flower

Dark and pale green for foliage

Pale green tape

#16 and #20 stem wire

Vine has 2 buds, 2 flowers, 3 leaves.

Center 1: Blue or violet [3]
#28   3″ of bare wire, ½″ loops wrapped once, 3″ bare wire. Bead each hanging stem in color for 1″. Twist wires below beads. Spiral beaded stems.

Center 2: Pale green [5]
#26   1″ of bare wire, 1″ loop narrowed. Twist three times directly under beads. Cut away starting wire. Push 1″ of beads close to loop. Cut away 2″ of free wire.

Center 3: String on the following color pattern:
#28   tern: [2]
3 blue, 4 white, 1″ blue, *4 white, 6 blue, 4 white, 1″ blue. *7 times. (End with 4 white, 3 blue.)

Make *each* loop in the following pattern:

3 blue, 4 white, 1″ blue, 4 white, 3 blue. Twist wires twice and continue in this pattern until there are 8 loops, all on one wire. Narrow all loops.

Petals: White
#26   Basic 1⅛″   Semipointed [5]
          Rows 7   top and bottom

Calyx: Pale green [1]
#28   2″ of bare wire, 10-bead loop wrapped once. Make a point on top of the second loop. Wrap once more; point this loop also. Make 6, all on one wire, leaving a short space between sets, to fit around stem.

Leaf Buds: Pale green   [2]
#28   1″ of bare wire, 1″ loop wrapped once. Make a point at top of second loop. Make 3 on one wire. Twist the beginning wire tightly under the loops. Cut away the beginning wire close to the loop. Push ½″ of beads close to the loop. Cut away 2″ of free wire. Pull rounded loop slightly away from pointed loop.

Leaves: Dark green   [3]
#26   Make a bottom basic with 2 long loops instead of one.

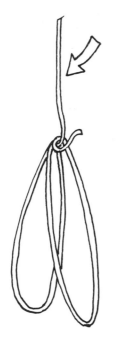

Basic 1¼″   Both ends pointed
Rows 5   (Basic count is in pale green.)

(Make a top basic without beads and add the basic count in pale green to the top basic wire.) Before cutting the petal free, continue with the beads on the feed wire, and loop back and forth in the spaces between petals with beads. Leave 1″ of beads on the feed wire. Cut away 2″ of free wire.

Assembly of Flower:
a. Twist the hanging wires of Center 1 together.
b. Twist the hanging wires of Center 2 together. Join to Center 1 and twist once more.
c. Place the 2 units of Center 3 around under the previous 2 centers and twist all wires together.
d. Tape the hanging wires.
e. Bind on to a short piece of #20 stem wire.
f. Bind the petals directly under centers, spacing evenly around.
g. Bind on calyx directly under flower.
h. Thin out and taper hanging wires, and tape to stem.
i. Repeat for other flower.

Assembly of Vine:
a. One bud is taped to top of #16 wire.
b. Tape on 1 flower 1½″ below.
c. Continue as diagramed.

PEONY

Materials

#26 silver wire
#32 binding wire
Yellow for centers
Pink, red, or yellow crystal plus white for flower
Medium green for foliage
Light green tape
#16 stem wire

Centers:	Yellow	4—2″ loops, all on one wire	[1]
Petals:	Color		
ROW 1:*		Basic 1″ Pointed top	[2]
		Rows 3 Round bottom	
	*Branch method	2—2½″ loops on each side	
ROW 2:	Repeat Row 1.		[4]
ROW 3:	Put one strand of white on the wire. For each petal add 3¼″ of color.		
	Repeat Row 1.		[5]
ROW 4:	Put one strand of white on the wire. For each petal add 7″ of color.		
		Basic 1″ Round top	[5]
		Rows 5 Pointed bottom	
	*Branch method	1—3″ loop on each side	
ROW 5:	Solid white	Basic 1″ Round top	[8]
		Rows 7 Pointed bottom	
Calyx:		Basic 1″ Pointed top	[4]
		Rows 7 Round bottom	
Leaves:		Basic 1″ Pointed top	[7]
		Rows 7 and bottom	

Assembly:

a. Tape the top 3″ of a stem wire.
b. Cluster the center loops and tape them to the top of the stem.
c. Bind on Row 1 with back of petals facing the center.
d. Tape the bindings for ¾″.
e. Bind on Row 2, spacing evenly around stem, as in c.

f. Tape the binding.
g. Bind on Row 3 in the same manner. Also repeat for Row 4.
h. Bind on Row 5 with front sides up in same manner.
i. Add the calyx squarely around the stem, tightly under the flower.
j. Taper and shorten all hanging wires and tape down stem.

k. Tape a 6″ piece of stem wire and tape one leaf to the top.
l. Tape one on each side ½″ below.
m. Add the remaining leaves, all ½″ below one another and pointing upward.

n. Add this stem to the main branch with #32 wire, 4″ under the flower.
o. Tape down remainder of stem.

Shaping:

Tips of Row 1 will be curved over the centers.
Row 2 arches over the center.
Row 3 also arches toward the center, but the tips are bent back.
Row 4 stands straight out, horizontally, with tips bent down.
Row 5 is also out horizontally.

PINE CONE

Materials

#25 gold wire
Brown or tortoise crystal.
Brown tape
#16 stem wire

All petals are round top and bottom.

Row 1:	Basic 7	[6]
	Rows 5	
Row 2:	Basic 7	[5]
	Rows 7	
Row 3:	Basic 9	[6]
	Rows 9	
Row 4:	Basic 11	[7]
	Rows 9	
Row 5:	Basic 13	[14]
	Rows 9	

Assembly:

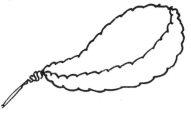

a. Arc-shape all petals. Tape a 12″ piece of stem wire.
b. Tape 2 of the first size petals to the top, facing each other.

c. All petals are front sides out. Tape 4 of the same size ½″ under, to fit evenly around stem.
d. Tape each size in order, overlapping the base of the petals, to provide a good fit. All rows are ½″ under each other.
e. The final size has 7 petals on one row and 7 petals on the final row.
f. Tape down remainder of stem.

RANUNCULUS

Materials

#28 green wire for centers
#25 gold wire for entire flower
#32 binding wire
Black for centers
Cut crystal in any color
Dark green for foliage
Dark green tape
#16 stem wire

Centers:	Black	5—1⅜" loops, all on one wire	[1]

Petals: Split basic

ROW 1:	Basic 6	Round top	[3 units]
	Rows 5	Pointed bottom	
ROW 2:	Split basic		
	Basic 8	As above	[6 units]
	Rows 5		
ROW 3:	Split basic		
	Basic 10	As above	[5 units]
	Rows 7		
ROW 4:	Split basic		
	Basic 12	As above	[5 units]
	Rows 7		

Calyx:	5—12-bead loops wrapped once with 2 beads between units, all on one wire	[2]

Leaves:	Basic 12	Pointed top	[2]
	Rows 13	Round bottom	

Assembly:

a. Set 1 loop of the center up, with 4 spaced around it. Bend tips back. Twist hanging wires.

b. Hook stem wire through. Close hook.

c. Tape for ½".

d. Bind on the first row of petals, spacing evenly around.

e. Tape bindings.

f. Add each size row, in turn, in the same manner.

g. Point the outer loop of the calyx and bind in position, just under flower head.

h. Taper and shorten all hanging wires. Tape down stem.

i. Tape the leaves 2" under the flower, opposite each other.

j. Tape down remainder of stem.

Shaping:

The first row of petals is upright.

The second row angles up so the tips are even with the first row.

Each succeeding row angles up so that all tops of all petals are even.

Press the calyx against the flower.

The leaves nestle close to the stem with the tips bent back.

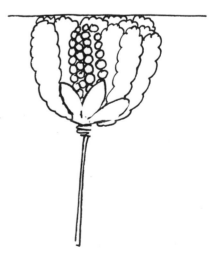

RHODODENDRON

Materials

#28 silver wire for flowers
#26 silver wire for foliage
#32 binding wire
Pink, purple, or white crystal for flowers
A few strands of red for stamen
Light and dark green for foliage
Light and dark green tape
#14 stem wire

Centers: With color on the wire, for each center add 1″ of red. 1″ loop in red, plus 3–12-bead loops in color, all on one wire [18]

Petals: Basic 6 Round top [90 in all]
Rows 7 Pointed bottom
5 per flower
Open all basic loops close to the petal and use as a single wire stem.

Leaves: Light green
Basic 1″ [3]
Rows 9

First 5 rows are pointed top and bottom. The remaining are round top and bottom.
Basic 1¼″ As above [3]
Rows 9
Dark green
Basic 1½″ As above [3]
Rows 9
Basic 2½″ As above [4]
Rows 11
First 7 rows are pointed top and bottom. The remaining are round top and bottom.
Lace if necessary.

Assembly:

a. Place 3 petals face up and 2 face down, on top of one another. Twist all hanging wires. Open the petals to form a cone shape.
b. Insert a center unit and tape the stem with light green tape. Make 18 florets this way.
c. Twist the bottom 1″ of 3 stems together as a unit.
d. Tape a full length of stem wire. Tape 3 small light green leaves to the top in a triangular position. Use light green tape.
e. Add the three large light green leaves 1″ under.
f. Bind on 3 petal units 1″ under, one at a time, spacing evenly around.
g. Tape the bindings with dark green tape.
h. Bind on 3 more petal units just under these, in the same manner.
i. Add 3 small dark leaves 2″ under the flower in a triangular position. Tape with dark green tape.
j. Add 2 large dark green leaves 1″ under on one side of the stem.
k. Add the 2 remaining leaves on the opposite side of the stem.
l. Tape down remainder of stem.

ROSE CASCADE

Materials

#26 silver wire
Any color for flower
Medium green for foliage
Dark green tape
#18 stem wire

Each spray consists of 4 small buds, 1 large bud, 2 flowers, 14 leaves.

Small Bud: | Basic 4 | Triple split basic
| Rows 7 | Pointed top
| | Round bottom

Large Bud: | Basic 5 | As above
| Rows 9 |

Flower:
UNIT #1 | Basic 4 | As above
| Rows 7 |
UNIT #2 | *Basic 5 | [4 per flower]
| Rows 9 |
| | Each petal is separate and round top and bottom. *Reverse basic.

Calyx: | Make 1 for each bud and each flower. 5—12-bead loops, all on one wire

Leaves:
#1 | Basic 5 | Semipointed top [7]
| Rows 7 | Round bottom
#2 | Basic 7 | As above [7]
| Rows 9 |

Assembly of Flowers and Buds:

a. Bud triple unit (3 petals in all) is assembled with the front sides of petals out and the tips all touching at the top.
b. The calyx is pressed against the bottom of the bud.
c. The flowers have the Unit 2 petals spaced evenly around Unit 1, and all hanging wires are twisted together.
d. Calyx is placed in position just like the bud.
e. Tape all hanging stems.

Assembly of Spray:

a. Tape a bud to the tip of the stem wire.
b. Tape on one leaf ½" down.
c. Continue working down the stem, alternating sides, in the following manner: 1 leaf; 1" under 1 flower; ¼" under 1 leaf; 1" under 1 bud; ¼" under 1 leaf.
d. Attach 1 flower at this point with 1½" of flower stem standing beyond the stem wire. This has 1 small and 1 large leaf on its own stem.
e. Continue along main stem for 1" and attach a second side branch exactly like d.
f. Final side branch has a small bud at the tip and a large bud where branch and main stem meet. Add final leaves at this point.
g. S curve entire branch.

RUDBECKIA

Materials

#26 silver wire
#32 binding wire
Topaz crystal for center dome
White, red, or yellow chalk for petals
Medium green for foliage
Dark green tape
#16 stem wire

Center:	Dome petal		
	Basic 5	Round	[1]
	Rows 15		
Petals:	Split basic		
	Basic 1″	Pointed top	[6]
	Rows 5	and bottom	
Leaves:	Basic ¾″	Pointed top	[3]
	Rows 15	and bottom	
Calyx:	4—10-bead loops wrapped once with 3 beads between loops, all on one wire		[1]

Assembly:

a. Join the hanging wires of the dome together under the petal. Twist securely several times.
b. Hook on the stem wire. Close the hook.
c. Tape for ½″.
d. Bind on the petals one at a time to fit evenly around.
e. Tape down the stem.
f. Tape the calyx in position.
g. Tape the leaves 5″ under the flower in a triangular position.

Shaping:

All the petals have a deep arc, bent downward.
The bottoms of the leaves hug the stem. Tops are bent out.
Press the outer loops of the calyx against the flower and pull the inner loops downward.

SALVIA

Materials
#28 red enameled wire
Red crystal
Brown tape
#16 stem wire

Start with 2″ of bare wire. 2–1″ 3-row cross-over petals made opposite each other, all on one wire. Set the 2 petals over one another, with the bare wire on the inside. Twist the end wires.   [41]

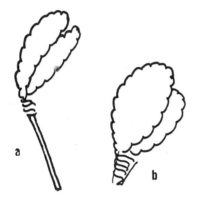

Assembly:
a. Tape the bare-wire stems of all florets. Tape as close to the beads as possible.
b. Tape a full length of stem wire.
c. Tape 2 florets to the top with ½″ of stem showing.
d. Tape 3 florets ½″ under to fit all around stem; ½″ of stem shows on each floret.
e. Add 3 more in the same manner.
f. Add 4 for each of the next 2 rows, then add 5 for each row.
g. Tape down the stem after the last row is attached.

Shaping:
Bend the floret stems away from the main stem, with the petals sitting on top of one another.

SCILLA

Materials

#26 silver wire for flowers and leaves
#28 wire for centers
#34 lacing wire
Any color for flower, with centers matching flower
Medium green for leaves
Dark green tape
#16 stem wire

Flower: Basic ¾″ Pointed top   [6]
            Rows 5   Semipointed bottom

Centers: 4—¾″ single beaded units, Method II

Bud 1:   Same count as flower.   [3]

Bud 2:   Same count as flower. Tips are laced together.   [3]

Leaves: Basic 3″ Pointed top   [5]
            Rows 5   Round bottom

Spray has 6 flowers, 2 buds, 5 leaves.

Assembly of Flower:

a. Place 3 petals on top of one another face up, 3 face down.
b. Twist all hanging wires twice.
c. Insert centers and twist again.
d. Face the petals upright with back sides facing into center.
e. Buds are assembled the same way.
f. Tape all hanging stems.

Assembly of Spray:

a. Tape a #16 stem wire.
b. Tape one flower with the stem extending 1″ beyond the tip of the stem wire.
c. Tape second flower 1½″ below the first. All flowers and buds have ½″ of their own stem extending beyond the main stem.
d. Leaves are added at the base of the spray, all in one spot, evenly around stem.
e. Tape leaves on one at a time.

SCOTCH BROOM

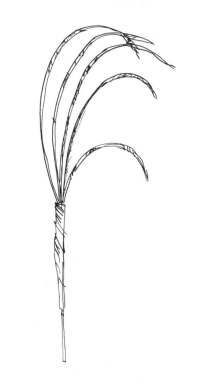

Materials
#26 silver wire
White floral tape

This is used to give graceful line and form to an arrangement.

a. Cut 6 pieces of #26 wire, varying the lengths from 6″ to 9″. Tape each piece very snugly.
b. Tape the bottom 2″ of all six pieces together.
c. Hold 1 piece loosely between thumb and forefinger where the cluster starts, and draw up and out in an arc shape.
d. Repeat for each of the others. Make as many clusters as needed for arrangement.
e. Each cluster is attached to a small piece of stem wire for ease when inserting into clay.

SMALL SUNFLOWER

Materials
#28 green wire for centers
#26 white enameled wire for petals
#26 silver wire for foliage
#32 binding wire
Black centers
Yellow chalk for petals
Medium green for foliage
Dark green tape
#16 stem wire

Center:	Dome petal		
	Basic 6	Round	[1]
	Rows 8		
UNIT 1	8—1½″ loops, all on one wire		[1]
UNIT 2	10—2″ loops, all on one wire		[1]
Petals:	Split basic		
	Basic ¾″	Pointed top	[3]
	Rows 5	Round bottom	
	Basic 1″	As above	[5]
	Rows 7		

Calyx:	8—2″ loops, all on one wire	[1]
Leaves:	*Branch method	
	Basic 1½″ Pointed top	[4]
	Rows 3 Round bottom	
	*2—2″ loops on each side	

118

Assembly:

a. Bring the end wires of the dome together under the petal. Twist securely.

b. Hook a #16 stem through. Close hook.

c. Bind on Unit 1 centers. Then bind on Unit 2 centers directly under.

d. Tape bindings.

e. Bind on the small petals one at a time, spacing evenly around.

f. Tape bindings for ½".

g. Bind on the larger petals, as in e and f.

h. Add the calyx firmly under the flower. Tape.

i. Add the 2 leaves 1" under the flower and opposite each other.

j. Add the remaining 2 leaves 1" under in the alternate position.

k. Tape down remainder of stem.

SNOWDROP

Materials

#26 silver wire
#32 binding wire
#34 lacing wire
White and medium green for flower
Medium green for leaves and calyx
Dark green tape
#16 stem wire

Large Petals: White	Basic ⅞" Rows 7	Round tops Elongated bottoms	[3]
Small Petals: White	Basic ⅜" Rows 3	Round tops Elongated bottoms	[3]
	Row 4: Last 6 beads in green		
	Row 5: First 6 beads in green		
	Rows 6 and 7 in white		
Center: Green	2–20-bead loops		[1]
Calyx:	5–1¼" loops Lace 3 beads down from top.		[1]
Leaves:	Basic 5" Rows 5	Pointed tops Round bottoms	[2]

Assembly:

a. Place the 3 small petals on top of one another, front sides up.

b. Twist all hanging wires twice, just below the beads.

c. Insert centers and twist once more.

d. Space petals evenly around centers with front sides out.

e. Hook a #16 stem wire through the back of the petals, and close hook.

f. Tape for 1".

g. Bind on larger petals one at a time with #32. Space evenly around.

h. Cut away binding wire and tape down stem.

i. Tape calyx around stem ½" below base of petals.

j. Tape on each leaf individually at same level. Leaf tip just reaches base of flower.

Shaping:

Curve stem wire so flower faces forward and downward.

Leaves face toward flower.

STEPHANOTIS

Materials
#25 gold wire
White irridescent crystal
Light green for calyx
Light green tape
#16 stem wire

12 flowers per stem.

Flower:
a. Start each unit with 2″ of bare wire. Push over 1″ of beads and let them float freely on the 2″ of bare wire.

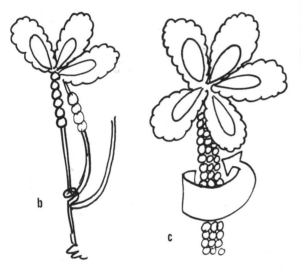

b. Make 3—½″ loops wrapped once, all on one wire. (Keep them close to one another.) Push over 1″ of beads. Turn petal with legs facing up. Twist the feed wire and the starting wire together under the legs in a complete turn. Push over 1″ of beads and turn petal with legs facing down. Bring bare wire between the second and third petal and out to the right.
c. Make 2—½″ loops wrapped once, on the same wire, and push over 1″ of beads. Turn petal with legs facing up. Twist feed wire and starting wire together in a complete turn. Cut away from the spool, leaving 8″ of bare wire. Cut away the starting wire.

Calyx:
a. String 2½″ of green on to the 8″ of bare wire.
b. Make 5½″ loops to fit around the base of the flower stem. The remaining 1″ of green is left for a stem.
c. Cut away from spool.

Assembly:
a. Set the 5 petals flat, in a circle.
b. Spiral the stem of the 4 white legs, like a barber pole.
c. Nest the calyx loops up around the base of this stem.
d. Twist 3 units together in a cluster. Make 4 clusters.
e. Tape a stem wire and tape one cluster to the top.
f. Add the remaining clusters 2″ under one another, down the stem.
g. Tape down the remainder of the stem.

Ming Tree

Dahlias—Giant Cactus Spray

Dogwood Branch

Red Band Lily

Sugar Plum Tree

Bougainvillaea

Double Painted Daisy

STRAWFLOWER

Materials

#25 gold wire
#32 binding wire
Two shades of any color for petals
Brown and yellow for centers
Brown tape
#18 stem wire

Leaves:
4/row crossovers
from 1½ – 2"

Centers:	Brown	Basic 4 Rows 8 Do not cut away basic wires.	Round top and bottom	[1]
	Yellow	6—1" loops, all on one wire		[2]
Petals: UNIT 1	Lighter color	6—1⅛" loops, all on one wire		[2]
UNIT 2		Repeat first row.		[2]
UNIT 3	Darker color	6—1¼" loops, all on one wire		[2]
UNIT 4		Repeat Row 3.		[2]

CALYX – 7 beads – 7 beads – make round w. pencil
Olive bead   make another 2 rows. Turn wires inside through
centre

Assembly:

a. Press all loops closed.
b. Set the center yellow loops face to face. Twist hanging wires.
c. Fan out the petals and straddle the brown petal across this circle.
d. Twist all hanging wires together underneath centers.
e. Hook on a #18 stem wire. Close hook.
f. Bind on the first row of petals, one on each side of the stem.
g. Tape bindings for ½".
h. Bind on successive rows in the same way.
i. Tape down remainder of stem.

Shaping:

Bend the tips of the yellow loops over the brown petal.
The first 2 rows of petals face up.
The third row is straight out.
The fourth row is bent down.

SWEET SULTAN

Materials

#28 silver wire for petals and center
#26 silver wire for foliage
#32 binding wire
Blue, purple, pink, or white crystal for petals
White for centers
Dark green for foliage
Dark green tape
#16 and #18 stem wire

Centers:

#28

Unit 1:	8–1″ loops, all on one wire	[3]
Unit 2:	12–1¾″ loops, all on one wire	[3]

Petals:

a. Knot the end of the wire. Push over ¾″ of beads. Leave 2″ of bare wire, then make 3 1″ loops, all on one wire. Push over ¾″ of beads.
b. Turn petal with legs up, draw feed wire around the first end wire, above the beads, as a basic turn, then push over ¾″ of beads.
c. Turn petal with legs facing down. Bring feed wire between the second and third petals and out to the right.
d. Make 2 more 1″ loops, push over ¾″ of beads.

e. Turn petal with legs up, draw feed wire around the first end wire as a basic turn. Twist end wires and cut free from spool.

The above procedure makes a petal with 5 loops and 4 vertical stems.

Calyx: 8–2½″ loops, all on one wire [1]

Leaves:	Basic 1″	Pointed top	[1]
	Rows 11	and bottom	
	Basic ¾″	As above	[4]
	Rows 9		

Assembly:

a. Spiral all center loops.
b. Set Unit 2 around Unit 1 and twist hanging wires.
c. Set legs of petals parallel to each other and spiral the top loops.

d. Tape a #16 stem and tape the center unit to the top.

e. Bind on 8 petals to fit evenly around. Tape binding.

f. Set the calyx in place firmly under the flower.

g. Bind and tape. Tape down remainder of stem. Make 3 stems.

h. Tape a 12″ piece of #18 stem and tape a large leaf to the top.

i. Tape 2 small leaves directly under, one on each side of stem.

j. Tape 2 more small leaves directly under, as in i. Make 3 stems.

k. Tape the bottom 4″ of the three flower stems together.

l. Bind on the 3 leaf stems in a triangular position around flower stem.

Shaping:

Center loops stand up at an angle, petals stand out straight.

Side leaves are angled upward.

TAMARIX

Materials

#25 gold wire for leaves and flowers
Multipink for flowers in crystal
Pale green for leaves
Yellow tape
#16 and #18 stem wire

Pattern: All on one wire: 15—8-bead loops with 2 beads between loops. On the same wire: 15—8-bead loops with 4 beads between loops. Continue on the same wire: 15—8-bead loops with 2 beads between loops. Fold the unit in half. Twist the hanging wires together. Gently spiral the entire unit.

[8 units per branch]

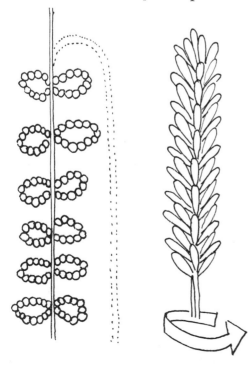

Leaves: All on one wire: 6—3″ loops with ½″ of beads between loops. On the same wire: 6—3″ loops with 1″ of beads between loops. Fold the unit in half. Twist all the way down, to spiral. Spiral each loop.

[6 per branch]

Assembly:

a. Tape a 6″ piece of #18 stem wire.

b. Tape 2 flowers to the top.

c. Tape one leaf 1½″ underneath.

d. Repeat *a*, *b*, and *c* for 2 more individual stems. (These are side branches.)

e. Tape a #16 stem wire.

f. Tape 2 flowers to the top.

g. Add 2 leaves at the same level, 1½″ under, on opposite sides of stem.

h. With #32 bind on one side branch 1″ below the leaves.

i. Tape the exposed wire.

j. Bind on a second branch 1″ below, on the opposite side of the stem.

k. Tape exposed wire.

l. Tape on a leaf at the joining point.

m. Bind on the final stem 1″ below joint.

n. Tape down remainder of stem.

TI LEAVES

Materials

#26 silver or #26 green wire
#34 lacing wire
2 shades of green
Dark green tape
Stem beads
#20 stem wire

Start with 3½ double strands on the wire, with the two shades strung at random.

Assembly:

a. Tape a #20 stem wire for 6″.

b. Slide on 4″ of stem beads.

c. Tape the stem beads in place.

d. At the 6″ end of the stem wire, bind the bare spool wire just under the beads.

e. Tape exposed wire.

f. Work around the 4″ of stem beads with a pointed top and round bottom until 21 rows are completed.

g. Lace as you work: ⅓ down from the top and ⅓ up from the bottom.

Shaping:

The leaf may be shaped as desired; it is usually curled back very sharply.

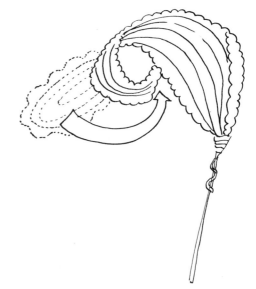

TIGERFLOWER

Materials

#25 gold wire for petals
#26 silver wire for foliage and centers
#32 binding wire
Topaz, orange, and yellow crystal for flower
Medium green for foliage
Light green tape
Stem beads
#16 and #20 stem wire

Centers: Start with 1″ of orange on the [1] wire, then add 4″ of green. 2–2″ loops in green. End the first hanging wire tightly under the loops and cut close to loop. Push over the orange. Leave 2″ of free wire and cut away from spool.

Center Cup: String the 3 colors together at random for 50″. [1]

| Basic 3 | Round top |
| Rows 18 | and bottom |

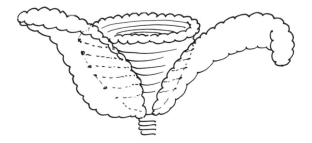

Cone-shape after the fourth row by shortening each row by 1 bead, and setting the row slightly above the previous row. Cut both basic wires and bend to back.

Inner Petals: Use the same multicolored beads. [3]

Basic 12	Round top
Rows 9	Semipointed
	bottom

Outer Petals: Use *one* of the colors as a solid. [3]

Basic 1″	Round top
Rows 15	Semipointed
	bottom

Leaves: Tape the top 2″ of a 12″ piece of #20 stem wire. Tape 6″ of stem beads in place *(using stem beads as a basic). Work 4 rows of pointed top and bottom. [2]

Assembly:

a. Draw the center loop and 3 inner petals down into the cup.
b. Twist all hanging wires.
c. Tape a #16 stem wire and tape the entire unit to the top.
d. Bind on the outer petals one at a time, spacing evenly around stem. Bind very firmly under cup. (Will form a triangle.)
e. Tape the bindings.
f. Tape down the entire stem.
g. Jewel the stem for 6″.
h. Add the leaves on either side of the stem, just under the jeweling.

Shaping:

The center loops will stand upright.
The inner petals lean on the cup with their tips bent back.
The outer petals hug the cup with their tips bent out.

TREE MALLOW

Materials

#25 gold wire for flowers and centers
#26 silver wire for foliage
#32 binding wire
Cut crystal in pink and yellow for the flower
Raspberry for the stamen
Light green and medium green for foliage
Light green tape
#16 stem wire

1 branch has 3 flowers, 8 buds, 3 leaves.

Centers: Yellow. Leave 2″ of bare wire. [1]
Make 6–10-bead loops, all on one wire. Cut
free from spool, leaving 2″ of bare wire. String
¾″ of raspberry on each leg. Twist the bare
wires and spiral the stem.

Petals: Triple split basic (two per flower)
    STEP 1:   Basic ½″   Round top
                Rows 3   Pointed bottom
Make a loop on the left side, slightly shorter
than the main petal. Make a loop on the right
side, slightly longer than the main petal.

    STEP 2:   Split the bottom basic loop and
                work each leg as follows:
                Basic ½″   Round top
                Rows 7   Pointed bottom
Cut free from spool, leaving 2″ of bare wire.

Leaves: Triple split basic. String the medium
green on wire and add light green for each
basic count (3 per stem).
                Basic 1″   Pointed top
                Rows 7   and bottom
Split the bottom basic loop and work each leg
as follows:
                Basic 5   Pointed top
                Rows 5   and bottom
Leave 1″ of beads for a stem.

Buds: Light green. 1″ crossover petal plus
4 1″ loops, all on one wire. Leave ½″ of beads
for a stem (8 per stem).

Assembly of Petals:

a. Hold 2 petals face to face and slide a center unit between.
b. Twist the hanging wires.
c. Tape the stem for 2″.

Assembly of Bud:

a. Set the 4 single loops around the crossover petal and use the first end wire to close the circle.

b. Twist twice close to the beads and cut away the feed wire.

c. Twist the bare-wire stems of 3 units together, two times. You will end with 2 triple units and 2 single units.

Assembly of Branch:

a. Tape 3 flowers and a unit of 3 buds to the top of a stem wire.

b. Twist a leaf and a bud together and tape to the stem 1" below.

c. Repeat once more.

d. Twist a leaf and a unit of 3 buds together and tape to stem 1" below.

e. Tape down entire stem.

Shaping:

Centers of flowers stand up straight.

Petals are at an angle with the tips of the larger petals bent back. Loops are opposite each other.

The 4 single loops of the bud are arched up with the tips pointed in.

TULIP, PARROT

Materials

#26 silver wire
#32 binding wire
Black for centers
Two shades of any color crystal or a color plus white
Dark green for foliage
Dark green tape
Stem beads
#16 and #20 stem wire

Centers: Start with 2" of bare wire. [5] Make a 6-bead loop. End with 2" of bare wire. String 1" of beads on each hanging wire. Twist bare wires below the beads.

Petals 1: Dark color. *Branch method. [3] Add 5½" of light for each petal. (Main part of petal will then be light.)

> Basic 1¾" Pointed top
> Rows 3   and bottom
> Add 3—4" loops on each side.
> Add 1—3½" loop on each side.

Petals 2: Dark color on wire. *Branch [3] method. Add 8" of light for each petal.

> Basic 2¾" Pointed top
> Rows 3   and bottom
> Add 3—5¼" loops on each side.
> Add 1—4½" loops on each side.

Leaves: "Using stem beads as a basic" [2] Tape the top 2" of a #20 stem wire. Slide on 5" of stem beads. Tape just under to hold beads in place. Work a pointed top, round bottom, until there are 13 rows in all. Lace ⅓ up from bottom and ⅓ down from top.

Assembly:

a. Cluster the centers together and twist hanging wires.

b. Tape to the top of a #16 stem wire.

c. Bind on petals of #1 to fit around the stem in a triangular position.

d. Tape the bindings.

e. Bind on Petals #2 in the open spaces just below #1. All front sides face out.

f. Thin out and taper the hanging wires.

g. Tape down entire stem.

h. Jewel stem for 5″.

i. Bind on each leaf individually, just where the jeweling ends, on each side of the stem.

j. Tape down remainder of stem.

Shaping:

Outer petals are arched up and out, in a deep arch.

Inner petals are arched more shallowly.

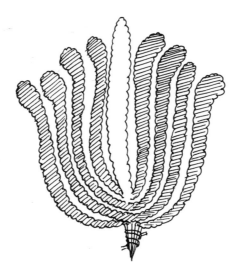

128

TULIP TREE BRANCH

Materials

#26 silver wire
#32 binding wire
Bright orange, bright yellow, light yellow crystal for flower
Light and medium green for foliage
Topaz for jeweling
Light green and brown tape
#16 and #20 stem wire

Centers:	Light yellow	1–4″ crossover petal plus 4–3¾″ loops, all on one wire	[1]
		12–3¾″ loops, all on one wire	[1]

Petals: String as follows for each petal:
7″ pale green; 3 orange beads; 2¼″ dark yellow; 3 orange beads; 2⅛″ pale green; 3 orange beads; 1⅞″ dark yellow; 5 orange beads; 1⅞″ light green; 5 orange beads; 1⅝″ dark yellow; 5 orange beads; 1½″ light green; 5 orange beads; 1⅜″ dark yellow; 2″ orange; 1″ dark yellow; 1⅝″ orange; 10 dark yellow beads; 1″ orange.

		Basic 1″ plus 3 beads Rows 14	Round top and bottom for 7 rows, then semipointed top	[6]
Calyx:	Medium green	Basic 1″ Rows 11 Work tightly to allow petal to curl up.	Round top and bottom	[3]
Small Leaves:	Medium green	Basic 1″ Rows 11	Pointed top and bottom	[4]
Large Leaves:	Tape a 10″ piece of #20 stem wire. Anchor the feed wire 4″ up from the bottom and use as a basic.			[2]
		Basic 1″ Rows 20	Pointed top and bottom	

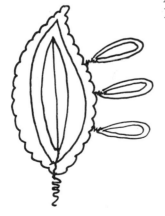

After 13 rows are completed, push over 2″ of beads, make a bare-wire loop close to the beads. Push over 8 beads tightly against the loop and make another bare-wire loop close to the beads. Push over 10 beads and make another bare-wire loop. Continue on, to complete the fourteenth row. Work around and use the bare-wire loops for additional basic turns. Work each turn as a point. One side of the leaf is straight. (When working between the side basics, press down between the points, to arc the sections.) Continue on to complete 20 rows.

The second leaf is worked in the same manner, but the bare-wire loops are made on the thirteenth row, so you will have a pair. All basic wires are bent to the back and cut away.

Assembly of Center:

a. Set the 4 single loops around the crossover petal.
b. Set the 12 loops around this and twist the bare wires.

Petal Shaping:

Press the thumb into the bottom of the petal and indent at this point. The bare wire is bent at 90° to this, the tips are bent back. This gives a tulip shape.

Assembly of 2 Small Leaves:

a. Twist the bare-wire stems of 2 small leaves together and lace across both at midpoint. Bend tips out.
b. Tape with light green for 2″.

Assembly of Branch:

a. Tape #16 stem wire. Tape the center to this wire.
b. Bind on 3 petals to fit evenly around.
c. Tape the bindings.
d. Bind on the next 3 in the open spaces below the first 3.
e. Tape for 1″.
f. Bind on the calyx, evenly spaced around. Tape down stem with brown.
g. Jewel stem for 3″, add the 2 small leaves opposite each other. Continue to jewel for 2″ more, add the large leaf, jewel for 2″ more.
h. Tape down stem.

Assembly of 2 Large Leaves:

a. Twist the two petals together firmly, under the leaf. Lace across both at midpoint. The straight edges are placed side by side.
b. Tape the stem for 2″ with green tape.

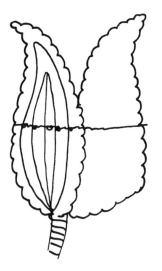

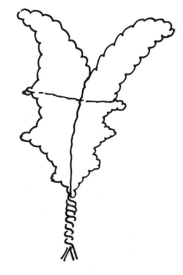

VALERIAN

Materials

#25 gold wire for flowers
#26 silver wire for foliage
Lavender, pink, or white crystal for flower
Medium and dark green for foliage
Light green tape
#16 and #18 stem wire
4 flowers, 2 buds, 9 leaves per branch

Flower
  Unit a: 5—1¼″ loops, all on one wire [1]

Flower
  Unit b: 7—1¼″ loops, all on one wire [1]

Flower
  Unit c: 9—1½″ loops, all on one wire [1]

Bud 1:   6—1″ loops, all on one wire   [1]

Bud 2:   String as follows: 10 green   [2]
beads; 4 colored beads; *20 green, 4 colored;
repeat from * 4 times, ending with 10 green
beads.
  Make 5 loops, all on one wire: 10 green, 4
color, 10 green.

Leaves: Start with dark shade on wire,
then add light. Basic amounts are light and
final 2 rows are light.
          Basic 1″   Pointed top   [9]
          Rows 7   and bottom

Assembly:

a. Cluster 1 of Unit a. Looks set straight up.
b. Set 1 of Unit b around this and twist
hanging wires.
c. Add 1 of Unit c around this and twist
hanging wires. Repeat for all 4 flowers.
d. Tape the bare wires for 2″.
e. Cluster the loops of the buds in the same
manner and tape. 1 bud will be solid color
and 2 in double color.

f. Tape 3—8″ pieces of #18 stem wire. On
one, tape a leaf to the top, and 4 more 1″ under one another on alternate sides of the stem.
g. On 2, tape a flower to the top with 1″ of
stem showing. Add a bud 1″ under with ¾″
of stem showing. Add a leaf 1″ below.
h. Tape a full length of #16 stem wire and
tape 2 flowers to the top, with 1″ of stem
showing.
i. Add a solid color bud ¾″ under with 1″
of stem showing.
j. Add 2 leaves opposite each other 1″ down.
k. Add a flower and bud stem 1″ down on
one side.
l. Add the leaf stem 1″ below, on opposite
side.
m. Add the final flower and bud stem 1″
down.
n. Tape down remainder of stem.

Shaping:

All flowers and buds face up.
All leaves are horizontal.

VERONICA

Materials

#25 gold wire for florets
#26 silver wire for foliage
Blue, pink, or white crystal or chalk for flower
Medium green for leaves
Light green tape
#16 and #20 stem wire

Unit 1: Knot the end of the wire. Push over 8 beads. Allow 2″ of bare wire and make an 8-bead loop. Push over 8 beads; make a 2″ bare-wire loop, tightly against the 8 beads. This will be the stem of the next section.

Push over 8 beads, make an 8-bead loop, then push over 8 beads. Make a 2″ bare-wire loop. Repeat this until 5 petals are completed.   [3]

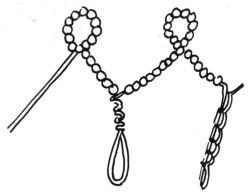

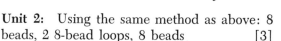

Unit 2: Using the same method as above: 8 beads, 2 8-bead loops, 8 beads   [3]

Unit 3: Same method: 9 beads, 3—8-bead loops, 9 beads   [3]
Repeat for 6 petals.

Unit 4: Same method: 10 beads, 4—8-bead loops plus 1—20-bead loop, 10 beads   [10]
Repeat for 6 petals.

Leaves: Tape a 10″ piece of #20 stem   [2] wire. Anchor the feed wire 4″ up from the bottom. Use the stem as a basic and work 14 rows of pointed top and bottom. Lace through center.

Basic 2½″
Rows 14

Trim off all but 1″ of the bare-wire loops of all the units.

Assembly:

a. Tape a #16 stem wire.
b. Hold a Unit 1 to the top of the stem with the bare wires hanging down the stem. Fit evenly around the top. Tape to the stem.
c. Add a second unit 1½″ under this in the same manner.
d. Continue down the stem, taping on one unit at a time, adding the last Unit 1.
e. Add each unit ½″ under another until you reach Unit 4. At this point join each unit ¼″ below another.
f. Tape the 2 leaves just under the flower, on opposite sides of the stem.

Shaping:

All florets angle up and out.
Leaves stand up straight with tips bent back.

WATER LILY

Materials

#25 gold and #26 silver wire
#32 binding wire
Yellow crystal for centers
Any color crystal for petals
Dark green for foliage
Dark green tape
#16 stem wire

Centers:

#25 gold

PART 1:	Basic 3	Round top	[1]
	Rows 6	and bottom	
PART 2:	8—1" loops, all on one wire		[1]
PART 3:	10—1⅜" loops, all on one wire		[1]

Petals:	Split basic		
#26 silver	Basic ¾"	Semipointed top	[5]
	Rows 5	and bottom	
	Basic 1"	As above	[5]
	Rows 7		

Sepals:	Basic 1½"	Pointed top	[4]
	Rows 9	Round bottom	

Pads: Start with 4 double strands of green on #32 binding wire. Cut 6—12" pieces of #26 wire. Cut 2—16" pieces of #26. Twist the 2 longer pieces together as one, for 10". Twist all pieces together as one, for 7". Fan out the 7 stems into a circle. These become the frame of the pad.

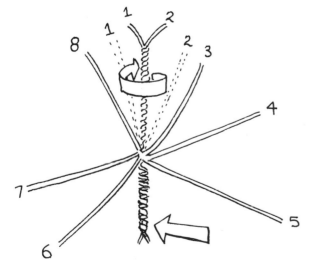

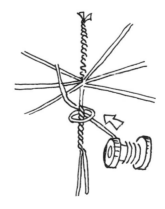

a. Anchor the feed wire around the twisted stems and bring up on the left side of the frame leg, which is the open 6″ at the top.

b. Go around this leg like a basic turn, close to the center point of the frame.

c. With 1 bead between each leg, repeat around the frame. Keep the frame flat. There is no need to count beads between the frame legs. Simply fill the space with enough beads to keep frame flat.

d. Continue to work around the frame until the open 2 wires of the starter leg are reached.

e. Make a complete turn around one side of this opening and go back in the direction from which you came.

f. When the opposite side of the opening is reached, repeat e.

g. Continue to work back and forth until the V measures 2½″. String enough beads on each leg of the V to cover each side, down to the point. Draw the feed ends down to the point of the V and bring them to the back of the petal. Twist ends and bend back. Cut all top end wires and bend back as a usual basic.

h. Tape the stem all the way down.

i. Jewel for 5″.

j. Tape to a 6″ piece of stem wire.

Assembly:

a. Tape a #16 stem wire.

b. Bring the end wires of Center–Part 1 together, under the petal. Set Part 2 around this and twist the end wires. Repeat for Part 3.

c. Tape all units to the top of a stem.

d. Bind on the first size of petals, spacing evenly around.

e. Tape the bindings for ½″.

f. Add the next size petals in the same way.

g. Taper and shorten hanging wires.

h. Bind on the sepals to face squarely around stem.

i. Tape down the entire stem.

j. Jewel for 6″.

Shaping:

First row of loops hugs the sides of the center.

Next row stands away slightly.

First row of petals is out horizontally with tips bent up.

Second row of petals is slightly arched.

Sepals stand out horizontally with tips bent up.

Spiral the jeweled stem of each flower and the pad around a pencil or dowel.

WINDFLOWER

Materials

#26 silver or #25 gold wire for entire flower
#32 binding wire
Main color plus a contrast in crystal
Brown crystal for centers
Dark green for foliage
Dark green tape
Stem beads
#20 stem wire

Spray has 3 flowers and 5 leaves.

Petals: Basic 6   Round top   [6]
Rows 9   Pointed bottom
Last 2 rows are in contrasting color.

Centers: Basic 4   Round top   [1]
Rows 7   and bottom
Last 2 rows are in contrasting color.

Leaves: *Branch method
Basic 1½″   Pointed top   [5]
Rows 3   Round bottom

*Add 1 loop each side almost as tall as the basic.

Add 1 loop each side half the height of the basic.

Bead each hanging stem of two leaves for 1½″. Bead the other three for 2½″. (Be sure to twist the hanging wires, so beads won't slide off.)

Assembly:

a. Place 3 petals face up and 3 face down, on top of one another.
b. Twist all hanging wires close to beads.
c. Fan out petals with front sides up.
d. Straddle center across flower.
e. Twist all hanging wires together once more.
f. Hook a #20 stem wire through the back of the flower.

g. Close hook.
h. Thin out and shorten the hanging wires to 1″ length.
i. Tape the hanging wires to the stem for 1¼″.
j. Jewel under the flower for 1¼″.
k. Bind bare wire closely under the jeweling and cut away.
l. Push stem beads on to each stem at a different height: 5″, 5½″, 6″.
m. Tape under stem beads, catching the last bead into the tape.
n. Bind all 3 flowers together with #32 wire, just where the stem beads end.
o. Bind on each leaf with #32 wire, all at the same level, evenly around the stem.
p. Tape exposed wire and tape down remainder of stem.

WOOD ROSE

Materials

#25 gold wire
Wheat plus topaz or brown
#26 green wire
#32 binding wire
#34 lacing wire
Wheat, topaz, and brown crystal
Brown tape
#16 stem wire

Unit 1:	Wheat color			
#26 green	Basic 5	Pointed top	[4]	
	Rows 11	and bottom		
	*Do not cut away top basics.			
	*Lantern assembly			

Unit 2:	Wheat color			
#25 gold	Basic 1″	Pointed top	[5]	
	Rows 15	Round bottom		

Unit 3:	Topaz or brown			
#25 gold	Basic 1″	Pointed top	[5]	
	Rows 13	Round bottom		

Arc petals gently by pressing thumb against wrong side of each petal and pushing outward. Proceed as in lantern assembly.

Assembly of Flower:

a. Make a ½″ hook on an 18″ piece of #16 stem wire.
b. Hook into lantern assembly. Close hook.
c. Tape for 1″.
d. Place a petal of Unit 3 behind a petal of Unit 2, with wrong sides together.
e. Twist the hanging stems together 2 or 3 times. Gently curl the tips of *both* petals back over the darker petal. Shape the bottom into a deep S.

f. Repeat d and e for 5 sets.
g. Bind on each set one at a time with #32. Overlap slightly as you bind.
h. Tape down entire stem.
i. Jewel the stem with brown beads for 6″.

Finishing of Flower:

With #34 lacing wire, weave the petals together in the following manner:
a. Start at the right, halfway down.
b. Go inside, then back again to the outside, over *one* row of beads.
c. Slide the inside part of the stitch over several rows (like a basting stitch).

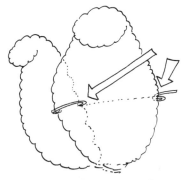

d. When all the petals are caught, pull the wires gently together and twist for ½″.
e. Cut away the rest of the wire and push the ½″ inside the flower.

ZINNIA, DAHLIA FLOWERED

Materials

5 STRANDS

#28 silver wire
#32 binding wire
Any color chalk or crystal for flower
Yellow crystal or chalk for centers
Dark green for foliage
Dark green tape
#18 stem wire

Centers:	6—¾" loops, all on one wire	[1]
Petals:	(4½")	
Row 1:	4—¾" loops wrapped once, all on one wire	[1]
Row 2:	6—1" loops wrapped once, all on one wire	[1]
Row 3:	8—1¼" loops wrapped once, all on one wire	[1]
Row 4:	7—1¼" loops wrapped twice, all on one wire	[1]
Leaves:	Basic 12 Pointed top Rows 9 Round bottom	[3]
Calyx:	4—10-bead loops, wrapped once, with 2 beads between loops, all on one wire	[1]

Assembly:

a. Tape an 8" piece of stem wire.
b. Tape the center to the top.
c. Bind on each size in order.
d. Tape the bindings for ½".
e. Add the calyx.
f. Tape down the stem.
g. Add the leaves 2" under the flower in a triangular position.

ZINNIA, OLD MEXICO

Materials

#25 gold wire for flower
#26 silver wire for foliage
#32 binding wire
#34 lacing wire
Orange and yellow crystal for petals
Medium green for foliage
Dark green tape
#16 stem wire.

Centers:	Yellow	3—3½″ 4-row crossovers, all on one wire	[2]
Petals:			

Row 1: Start with orange on the feed wire.

Basic 1¾″	Pointed top	[6]
Rows 7	and bottom	

Complete 5¾ rows. Estimate enough wire to complete petal and cut away from spool. String on enough yellow to finish the *row*. Match same amount on other side, then string on orange to complete the petal.

Row 2:

Basic 2¼″	Pointed top	[10]
Rows 5	and bottom	

Complete the first 3¾ rows and finish petal as above.

Row 3:

Basic 2¾″	Pointed top	[14]
Rows 5	and bottom	

Complete as in Row 2.

Leaf Stems: Tape a full length of #16 stem wire. Anchor the feed wire 5″ up from the bottom. Use the stem as a basic.

Basic 9	Pointed top
Rows 30	Round bottom

After 4th row, lace across center as you work. Start another petal 2½″ above the first leaf, on the same stem.

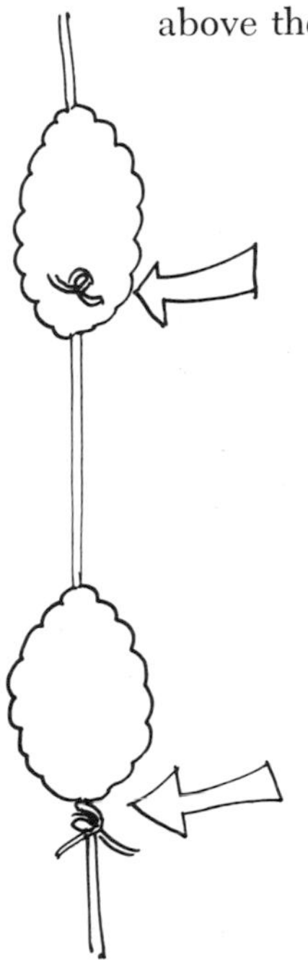

Basic 7	Pointed top
Rows 24	and bottom

Complete second leaf, lacing as first. Start another petal 2¼″ above second leaf, on same stem.

Basic 7	Pointed top
Rows 22	Round bottom

Lace as first leaf.
Tape the exposed wire between the petals.

Calyx:		4—2″ loops, all on one wire	[3]
Buds:	With green	5—2″ 3-row crossover petals, all on one wire	
(2)	With orange	4—1½″ loops, all on one wire	

Assembly of Bud:

a. Arc-shape the crossovers, with bare wire on the inside. Tips point to each other. Cluster the orange loops, set them into the green.
b. Tape one bud to the top of the leaf stem.
c. Tape the second bud between the two larger leaves.

Assembly:

a. Twist the hanging wires of both center units. Form the 2 units into a circle.
b. Hook a #16 wire through and close hook.
c. Tape for ½″.
d. Bind on the Row 1 petals, one at a time with #32 wire. Space evenly around stem.
e. Tape bindings for ¾″.

f. Bind on each row in the same manner.
g. Bind on the calyx, one at a time, firmly under the flower.
h. Taper and shorten all hanging wires.
i. Tape down remainder of stem.
j. Bind the leaf stem to the flower 6″ below the flower head.

Shaping:

First row nestles against the centers. Tips of petals are bent out.
Form the remaining rows more or less the same way.
Press the calyx gently against the flower head.
The leaf stem leans away from the flower, at the top.

ZINNIA, PEPPERMINT

Materials
#26 silver wire
#32 binding wire
Speckled chalk beads in white and red, or
white and orange, with matching solid color
Dark green for foliage
Dark green tape
#16 stem wire

solid color for basic amount on the next two petals. Use same count as first petal.

Row 2:	Solid color on feed wire. Same method as Row 1.			
	Basic ⅞″	Pointed top		[4]
	Rows 3	and bottom		
	Use speckled for basic amount.			
Row 3:	Solid color on feed wire. Same method as Row 1. Add speckled for *all* basic amounts.			
	Basic 1″	Pointed top		[4]
	Rows 3	and bottom		
Calyx:	4—1″ loops wrapped once loosely with three beads between sets, all on one wire			[1]
Leaves:	Split basic.			
	Basic ¾″	Pointed top		[1]
	Rows 9	Round bottom		
	Basic ¾″	As above		[1]
	Rows 11			

Assembly:

a. Cluster the center and twist the hanging wires.
b. Hook on a **#16** stem wire. Close the hook.
c. Bind on the first row, spacing petals evenly around stem.
d. Tape bindings for ¾″.
e. Bind on the next rows in the same manner.
f. Add the calyx closely under the flower and bind on tightly.
g. Taper and thin out hanging wires.
h. Tape down entire stem.
i. Add the small leaf 2″ under the flower with tape.
j. Add the larger leaf 1″ below on the opposite side with tape.

Shaping:

First row is upright with tips bent out.
The next two rows follow the same shape.
The outer loop of the calyx is pointed and pressed up against the flower. The inner loop is bent down toward stem.
Leaves are arched at midpoint.

Bud:	Speckled	4—1½″ loops, all on one wire	[1]
	Green	4—1½″ loops, all on one wire	[1]
Leaves:	Basic ¾″	Pointed top	[2]
	Rows 9	Round bottom	

Assembly of Bud:

a. Form speckled loops into a circle.
b. Surround with green loops.
c. Twist all hanging wires directly below the beads.
d. Hook a #18 stem wire through bottom.
e. Shorten hanging wires and tape down stem.
f. Tape on leaves opposite one another, 1″ below bud.
g. Join bud stem to main stem ¾″ below leaves.
h. Bind together with #32 binding wire.
i. Tape down remainder of stem.

6

Flower Arranging

As far back as the fifth century, vases of flowers were used for decoration. Today, manmade flowers of all types and materials are used as an integral part of the decor. The array of these flowers is extensive, and the kinds of material used too numerous to mention. Beaded flowers are especially beautiful, and their everlasting quality makes them most desirable.

To derive the greatest pleasure from the many hours you have put into making your flowers, you will want to arrange them yourself. Your own personal taste will be a deciding factor in the type of arrangement you make. Once you have acquainted yourself with the basics, the sky is the limit!

Basic Principles of Design

There are six basic principles of design: balance, dominance, contrast, rhythm, proportion, and scale. No matter what type of arrangement you make, these principles will apply.

BALANCE   A balanced arrangement gives a feeling of stability. The arrangement does not appear to be leaning to either side, forward, or backward. Balance can be either actual (symmetrical) or visual (asymmetrical). A symmetrical balanced arrangement is the same on each side of a central axis. An asymmetrical arrangement employs different materials, colors, textures, sizes, or lines on each side of a central axis. Darker or brighter colors, coarser textures, and larger flowers all appear

heavier to the eye. For example, if three small pale pink flowers are used on one side of the central axis, one large dark maroon flower might be all that is necessary to balance the other side.

DOMINANCE   A point of interest, something that draws the eye to the arrangement, is achieved through dominance. The dominant area is usually kept to the bottom one third of the arrangement. Repetition of color, form, material, or line develops dominance.

CONTRAST   By using different materials, colors, forms, and lines you have contrast. Contrast is important, as it places emphasis on the dominant feature. Care must be taken not to use too much contrast because confusion will result. Not more than one third of the arrangement should be contrast.

RHYTHM   Rhythm carries the eye through the arrangement by using transition and repetition of materials. Transition can be achieved by using a bud in the top of the arrangement and graduating to a full-blown flower at the base of the container. A light color at the top graduated to a darker shade at the bottom will accomplish the same effect. Varying color, texture, and flower form will also give the desired effect. Be sure to carry the material over the rim of the container, as this incorporates the container as a part of the whole composition.

PROPORTION   The space the arrangement will occupy, the size of the flowers, and the size of the container should be considered in direct relation to one another. A good approximation to follow is one and a half times the width of a shallow container, or one and a half times the height of a tall container, with variation depending upon the above-mentioned factors.

SCALE   A size relationship should be established between the components, container, and accessories of the arrangement. Your own good judgment will help you with scale. For instance, you would certainly not mix stephanotis with a chrysanthemum arrangement.

The principles of design are interrelated. As you are working, you will see how one leads into another. However, when arranging beaded flowers, you have poetic license. You will find that you do not necessarily adhere to all the principles of design as strictly as you would with fresh flowers.

Color

Color is the most important element of design when arranging beaded flowers. An arrangement that lacks color harmony, no matter how skillfully executed, will be a disappointment. Most of us have a natural feeling for color, but at times a question does enter our mind. A simple color wheel is a most worthwhile investment and will answer your questions.

Take a few minutes before you start planning your arrangement to study the area the arrangement will occupy. Note the background. Now decide on a color scheme for your arrangement. Do you want to carry through the dominant color in the room or bring out an accent color? Possibly you will want to choose a contrasting color scheme.

A monotone (one color) arrangement can be very striking when placed in front of a contrasting background. Care must be taken not to place a monotone arrangement in front of a busy background, as it will be lost.

A monochromatic (varying shades of one color) arrangement utilizes the different degrees of color to emphasize the design. By using the lightest shade at the apex of the arrangement and the darkest shade at the base, you will also have rhythm.

An analogous (adjacent colors on the color wheel) arrangement should have three or more colors in the design. This scheme can be very effective when used to make a centerpiece. By placing the lighter colors to the top and sides and the darker colors to the center and base, you create a definite feeling of depth. One color should be dominant in the arrangement.

A complementary (opposite on the color wheel) arrangement should have one color dominant. A red and green, or blue and orange, color scheme are examples of direct complements.

A triad (colors spaced at equal distances apart on the color wheel) arrangement would encompass three colors. Varying shades of these colors can also be employed in the arrangement. This color scheme is most often used with informal arrangements as a large mixed bouquet. Be sure to use varying amounts of each color so that one does not predominate.

Basic Forms of Design

There are seven basic forms of design from which to choose. By familiarizing yourself with these designs you will be able to know at a glance what form will suit the space you wish to fill. Illustrated are diagrams of the seven basic forms: vertical, crescent, oval, horizontal, L-shape, hogarth, triangular.

You can divide your flowers into three categories: round, spike, and spray. Round flowers are the small sunflower, strawflower, water lily, wood rose, rose cascade, etc. Spike flowers include salvia, tamarix, cattail, gladiolus. Spray flowers are fern, autumn leaves, Scotch broom, indigo, etc. The spray flowers are often used as fillers in an arrangement. Certain flowers will fit into more than one category.

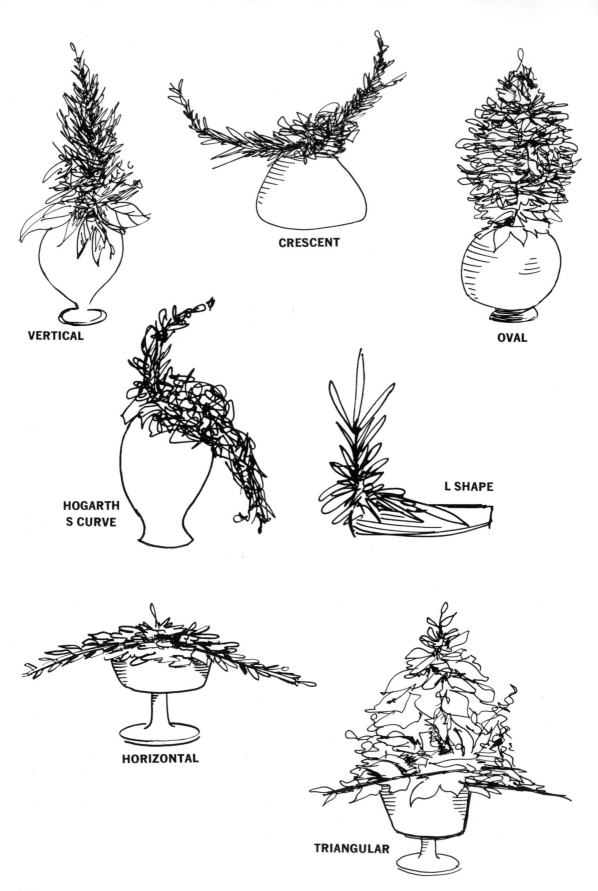

VERTICAL

CRESCENT

OVAL

HOGARTH S CURVE

L SHAPE

HORIZONTAL

TRIANGULAR

144

When making an arrangement, you will usually start with spike flowers to outline the general shape of the arrangement. They may also be used throughout the arrangement and can be used to define a particular line.

Containers

Your choice of container will depend upon the type of arrangement you are making, the flowers used, and the space it will occupy. The container is considered a part of the arrangement and should be coordinated with the other parts. The color of the container will depend upon the color scheme of the arrangement and the area it will be in. You may choose to repeat a color from the arrangement or to keep the container neutral. Use a container that will place the emphasis on the flowers, not on the container. The size of the container should be in scale with the size of the flowers and the space it will occupy. You certainly wouldn't put a sunflower in a bud vase and set in on a hearth.

The material used as a holder when arranging beaded flowers is nonhardening florists' clay. Pack the clay into the container, leaving a ½″ to ¾″ space at the top. If the clay is hard, work it in your hands for a few minutes or put it in a slow oven to soften. For an attractive finished appearance place sheet moss on top of the clay.

Certain containers will require special handling when being filled with clay. Tall vases need not be packed with clay; instead, fill a hollow cardboard tube with clay and fix it to the bottom of the container with Permagum or clay. If the vase is extremely tall and not transparent, you may want to add a few inches of marbles, pebbles, or sand for stability. A good way to handle tall transparent containers is to conceal the cardboard tube with sheet moss. Silver containers or any that require cleaning should have a liner. An inexpensive plastic bowl or heavy foil is very satisfactory as a liner. All transparent containers need a decorative liner of some kind.

Sheet moss is always attractive. Heavy foil not only serves the purpose of making an appealing liner but also allows you to lift the arrangement out of the container for ease of cleaning, without disturbing the flowers.

Accessories

Accessories, when used properly, can make an attractive addition to an arrangement. The accessory should always be in scale with the other parts of the arrangement. Remember that this addition will affect all the principles of design. The balance will be affected by the size, color, and texture of the accessory, as well as by its placement. It can complement the dominant feature and help to draw attention to the point of interest. It should be coordinated with the arrangement so as to appear as a part of the arrangement. If you find that an accessory you had in mind does not fit into this category, do not use it. Avoid using too many accessories, as confusion will result. By utilizing the lovely beaded fruit and charming beaded animals in this book you can be assured of having an accessory that will fit your arrangement perfectly.

Care of Beaded Flower Arrangements

Once you have completed your arrangement, there is a minimum of care necessary. A soft feather duster will keep it fresh for quite some time. However, the time will come when it will be necessary to wash your arrangement. The best way to do this is to fill a plastic dishpan or a sink with warm soapy water. (A mild detergent may be used.) Dip the arrangement head first into the solution and gently swish around. Rinse and let dry. If you are careful, this process can be done without removing the flowers from the container. This might be a good time, however, to add to or change your arrangement.

The most important point to remember about arranging is that it must please *you*. No two people will ever come up with the same arrangement.

7

Fruit

Beaded fruits were originally intended to be used as arrangement accessories. However, they were so lovely that we added many more designs and gave them a section of their own.

They look charming in a simple fruit bowl, but are particularly effective when layered on the epergne. They also make an interesting focal point when placed gracefully on a mirror in the center of a dinner table. The strawberry plant adapts beautifully to a strawberry-jam pot but may also be used without the foliage in a fruit grouping.

With a little ingenuity and imagination, you can vary your arrangement to reflect your own personality.

NOTE: If, for some reason, the suggested sizes of plastic fruit are not available to you, give it a try anyway. Check the required number of petals for the fruit. Make one of the petals but do not cut it free from the spool. If the instructions call for three petals, one of them should cover one third of the diameter of the fruit. Shape the petal against the form and judge the size. If it does not cover one third, alter the size by adding or subtracting rows. Do not change the basic count. After you have decided that the petal is right for the form, make a note of the size and continue with the instructions.

APPLE

Materials

#28 silver or #26 red enameled wire
Red crystal for apple
Dark green for foliage
Dark green tape
Plastic apple, measuring 2″ from top to bottom

Do not cut any basic wires.

Apple Petals:	Basic 1″	Pointed top	[2]
	Rows 14	and bottom	
	Basic 1″	As above	[2]
	Rows 16		
Leaves:	Basic 9	Pointed top	[4]
	Rows 9	Round bottom	

Assembly:

a. Twist the top basic wires of one small and one large petal together. Front side of petal faces out.
b. Repeat with the second pair.
c. Twist all four petals together, holding each pair face to face. Twist goes to wrong side of petals.

d. Cut away all but ¼″ of the twisted wire.
e. Insert the form with the bottom resting against the ¼″ of wire.
f. Bring the sides up over the apple and twist all wires together.
g. Tape the stem for 2″.
h. Tape the leaf stems for 1″. Tape a leaf on the top of the apple, front side up, with the leaf stem running up the apple stem; ½″ of leaf stem shows.

i. Repeat this with remainder of leaves, having one opposite another, on alternate sides of the stem.

BANANA

Materials

#25 gold wire
#32 gold lacing wire
Banana-yellow crystal
Plastic banana, 4½″ long
Do not cut any basic wires.

Petals:	Basic 3″	Pointed top	[3]
	Rows 13	and bottom	
	Open basic loop close to beads.		

NOTE: One petal may be spotted by picking up a brown bead at random, as you string.

Assembly:

a. Lace the 3 petals together at ⅓ down and ⅓ up, across the front side of the petals.
b. Gently bring the top points together and twist the end wires on the inside of the petals.

c. Cut away all but ¼″ of this wire.
d. Set petals around the form.
e. Twist bottom end wires together and cut away as above.
f. Push this twist to the inside of the form and complete the lacing by joining the first petal to the last.
g. Twist the ends of the lacing wire together and push to the inside.

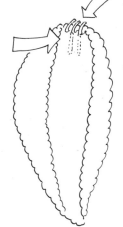

CRAB APPLE

Materials

#28 silver or #26 red enameled wire
Medium red crystal for fruit
Medium green for foliage
Dark green tape
Plastic apple, 1¼″

Petals: *Do not cut top basic wires.*

Basic ½″   Semipointed top   [4]
Rows 13   and bottom
Work tightly to curl petal.

Pip: Green Basic 3   Round top   [1]
Rows 5   and bottom
Trim and bend back both ends of
bare wire.

Leaves 1:   12-bead loop wrapped once.   [4]
Point the wrap.

Leaves 2:   Basic ¾″   Pointed top   [2]
Rows 7   Round bottom

Assembly:

a. Tape all leaf stems.
b. Twist 2 petals side by side at the top basic wires.
c. Repeat with second pair.

d. Hold one pair with back side facing you and string the basic twist up and over, through the spaces of the first row, of the green pip.
e. Push the pip tightly against the petal.
f. Repeat this with the second pair of petals, working in the opposite direction.
g. Pull tightly and twist both end wires together on the back side of the petals.
h. Trim all but ¼″ and insert the form.
i. Bring the sides up over the fruit to meet at the top.
j. Twist all wires together and tape for 2″.
k. Tape the small leaves to the stem ½″ up from the fruit with ½″ of stem showing.
l. Tape 2 large leaves above this opposite each other with ¾″ of stem showing. Front sides of leaves face up.

GRAPE CLUSTER

Materials

#28 silver wire
Purple, wine, or light green crystal
Brown tape
#16 stem wire
Sixteen 1″ Styrofoam balls dipped in Tintex to color them as close to the color of the beads as possible

Do not cut any basic wires.

Petals: Basic 4   Semipointed top
Rows 11   and bottom
After the seventh row, work very tightly to curve the petal. Make 3 petals per grape, 16 grapes per cluster: 48 petals in all.

Assembly of Grape:

a. Hold 2 petals with the wrong side facing you and twist the top basic wires together. Add a third petal. Be sure the beads are touching at this point.
b. Open the petals slightly to form a triangle. Push basic twists to inside.

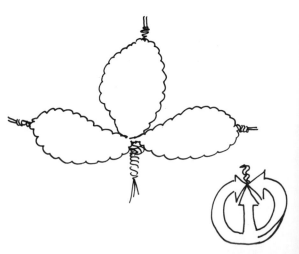

c. Cut away all but ½″ of this twist. Set a colored ball down on to the twisted wire.

d. Bring the petals up to meet over the top of the ball. Twist all wires.

e. Gently push the rows in place to fit the ball.

f. Tape the stems for 2″.

Assembly of Cluster:

a. Tape a #16 stem wire.

b. Tape 1 grape to the top with 1″ of stem showing. Grape faces up.

c. Tape 2 grapes side by side ¾″ below.

d. Add another 3 grapes ¾″ below.

e. Repeat with 3 more grapes ½″ under, and 3 more below that.

f. Add 4 grapes ¾″ below.

g. Tape down the stem.

Stems may be longer or shorter, to suit your taste.

KUMQUAT

Materials

#25 gold wire
Bright orange crystal
Brown tape
Plastic kumquat, 1½″ long

Do not cut top basic wires.

Petals: Basic 1″   Round top   [2]
         Rows 16   and bottom

After the seventh row, reduce each row by 1 bead. This will shape the petal to fit the form.

Assembly:

a. Twist the 2 petals together at the top basic wires, wrong side up.

b. Cut away all but ¼″ of this twist.

c. Insert the form.

d. Bring the petals together over the form and twist the end wires.

e. Tape the stem for 1″.

LEMON

Materials

#25 gold wire
Lemon-yellow crystal
Brown tape
Plastic lemon, 2″

Do not cut the top basic wires.

Petals: Basic 1″   Semipointed top   [4]
         Rows 13   and bottom

Assembly:

a. Twist the top basic wires together, as directed in lantern assembly.

b. Cut away all but ¼″ of the twisted wire.

c. Insert the form and bring the petals up around the lemon.

d. Twist all bare wires together.

e. Shape the petals downward to form a small protrusion at the bottom.

f. Trim all but 1″ of the top stem, and tape.

ORANGE

Materials
#25 gold wire
Orange crystal beads
Brown for the pip
Brown tape
Plastic orange, 1¾″

Do not cut any basic wires.

Petals: Basic ¾″   Semipointed top   [4]
            Rows 14   and bottom

Pip: Basic 3   Round top   [1]
            Rows 5   and bottom
Open the basic loop close to the beads, as a single wire. Draw both end wires together under the petal and string up through the center, to have them showing on the front side of petal.

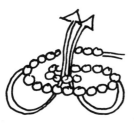

Assembly:
a. Hold 2 petals wrong side up and twist top basic wires. Be sure the beads are touching.
b. Repeat with the other 2 petals.
c. Twist all 4 petals together. Twist goes to wrong side of petals.
d. Cut away all but ¼″ of the twisted wire.
e. Insert form into petals with bottom against the ¼″ twist.
f. Bring the petals up over the orange and twist all wires.
g. Gently arrange rows to fit the form.
h. Tape the stem for 2″.
i. Slide the pip down the stem and hold it firmly against the orange.

j. Tape pip in place.
k. Spiral the stem down toward the orange.

PEARS

Materials
#25 gold wire
Pear-yellow crystal
Brown tape
Plastic pear, 2¼″ for "fruit bowl" and 1⅜″ for "partridge in a pear tree"

Do not cut any basic wires.

Pear for Fruit Bowl: Basic 10 Semipointed top [3]
                        Rows 21 Pointed bottom
                        After the thirteenth row, shorten the top by one bead. This will round out the top to fit over the form.

Assembly:
a. Assembly is the same as the orange, except there are only 3 petals.
b. Tape the stem for 1″.
c. Twist is made at the bottom point.

Pear for Pear Tree: Basic 6   Round top   [2]
                        Rows 17   Pointed bottom
                        Work tightly at the top to create a curl.

Assembly:
a. Twist the 2 petals together at the top basic wires. Twist goes inside.
b. Insert the form.
c. Bring the petals over the pear to meet.
d. Twist wires and shape the rows neatly around the form.
e. Tape the stem for 2″.

PINEAPPLE

Materials
#28 silver or #25 gold wire for petals
#26 silver wire for foliage
Orange, yellow, and medium green crystal for the fruit
Dark green for foliage
Green fabric dye
4″ Styrofoam egg

Flatten the top and bottom of the egg by pressing it and rubbing back and forth on a table top. Mix a small amount of dye and color the egg. Allow to dry overnight.

Petals: 15 in orange, 5 in yellow, 7 in green. 2–1″ loops plus a 1¼″ loop. Repeat until 4 sets are all on one wire. Close all loops and shape into a diamond.

Centers: 20 in green, 7 in orange. Leave a 1½″ top basic wire and a 3″ bottom basic loop.
Basic 3   Round top
Rows 6   and bottom
Cut feed wire even with the top basic wire. Open the bottom basic loop at the center.

Leaves: Basic 3″   Pointed top   [4]
            Rows 5   Semipointed bottom

            Basic 2½″   As above   [4]
            Rows 5

            Basic 1¾″   As above   [5]
            Rows 5

Assembly of Petals:
a. Set the green centers across the yellow and orange petals. Bring all hanging wires together at the center on the underside of the petal. Twist tightly for 1″ and cut even.
b. Set the orange centers across the green petals and complete as in a.
c. Twist the bare wires of the large leaves together, front sides in.
d. Add the leaves of the next size to fit all around.
e. Add the final size leaves, spacing evenly around.
f. Twist tightly.

Assembly of Fruit:
a. Bend the tops of all the leaves downward and press this cluster into the top of the form, tightly against the beads.
b. Press the yellow petals into the form, just under the flattened edge, to fit evenly around. Press the top loops down on to the form, under the leaves.
c. Press the orange petals into the form between two yellow ones, slightly overlapping the two colors. This forms a second row around the fruit and under the yellow.
d. Repeat this with a second row of orange petals under and between the upper row.
e. Press the green petals into the form in the same manner, all around the bottom of the form.

PLUM

Materials

#25 gold or #28 silver wire
Plum or purple crystal beads
Brown tape
Plastic plum, 1½″

Petals: Basic ½″ Semipointed top [3]
Rows 17 and bottom
Shorten the last 4 rows by 1 bead to curl petal.

Assembly:

a. Assemble in the same manner as the orange.
b. Tape the stem for 2″.

STRAWBERRY PLANT

Materials

#26 silver wire for foliage
#28 silver wire for flowers
#26 red enameled wire for *all* berries
Strawberry-red crystal
White crystal
Dark and light green for foliage
Dark and light green tape
#18 stem wire
Absorbent cotton balls

Flowers:	White	6—8-bead loops, all on 1 wire	[16]
		Set 1 into center and space 5 around it.	
Berries:	3 red each size	*Do not cut basic wires.* Work tightly to curl the round bottom.	
	3 light green each size	Make 3 petals per berry, light green for unripened berries, 9 per color.	
		Basic 7 Pointed top	
		Rows 9 Round bottom	
		Basic 9 As above, 9 per color	
		Rows 11	
Calyx for All Berries:	Light green	8—10-bead loops, all on one wire, per berry	[1]
Leaves:	Dark green	Basic 7 Round top	[6]
		Rows 13 Pointed bottom	
		Basic 5 As above	[3]
		Rows 11	
	Light green	Basic 5 As above	[12]
		Rows 9	

Assembly of Flower:

a. With light green tape, cover the hanging wires of each flower.

b. Tape 4–6″ pieces of stem wire.

c. Cluster 4 flowers and tape to the top of each stem.

Assembly of Berries:

a. Hold 2 petals together face to face and twist the top basic wires.

b. Add a third in a triangular position. Be sure the beads are touching at this point.

c. Open the petals to form a triangle with the twist on the inside. Trim all but ¼″ of the twisted wire.

d. Set in a wad of cotton the size of a pecan nut. Bring up the bottom basic wires to meet over the cotton. Twist the bare wires together.

e. Position the calyx tightly to the berry and tape for 2″ with dark green tape. Use light green tape for the green berries.

f. Tape 3–8″ pieces of stem wire. Tape 2 small berries to the top with 1″ of stem showing.

g. Add 2 large berries ½″ below. Tape down the stem.

h. Repeat this on one more stem using 1 small and 1 large berry.

i. Repeat for green berries.

Assembly of Leaves:

a. Tape the bare-wire stems of each leaf for 1½″. Use dark tape for the dark leaves and light tape for the light leaves.

b. Tape 4–8″ pieces of stem wire with light tape. Tape 3 light leaves to the top of each in a triangular position.

c. Tape 3–10″ pieces of stem wire with dark tape. Tape 1 small and 2 large dark leaves to the top of each, as above.

d. Place each stem into a container close to one another. All berries hang down. Leaves stand straight out. A strawberry jelly dish makes a perfect container for this plant.

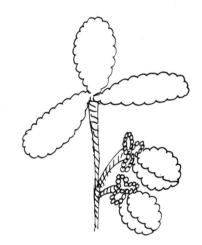

8

Trees

Sometimes it is easier and faster to make a single item for a special gift or a conversation piece. The chapter on trees was intended to satisfy this need.

The Ming and Oriental blossom trees are lovely focal points for any room. They are easy to make and can be completed with dispatch.

The espalier lends itself to the unusual or modern and can be a wonderful holiday piece when used as "a partridge in a pear tree."

The sugar plum is sheer delight for a party centerpiece or a child's room. When used for a sweet-sixteen or other birthday decoration, a ribbon can be attached to each plum and then spread on the table with a "favor" tied to each end. The sugar plum is also a whimsical gift to send to a college student. Assemble all leftover beads, mix the colors, and make a Pop Art tree. You can insert perfume or soap into each plum, as an added attraction.

The palm is also adaptable to many ideas. You can use it as part of a Japanese-style arrangement, or you might enjoy setting it into one end of a dish garden with little animals or insects below, like a miniature zoo.

For a real showstopper you can assemble branches, such as the dogwood or tulip tree, and make a life-sized tree. It is a major project but would be extremely effective.

ESPALIER TREE

Materials

#26 silver wire for leaves
Light and dark green
Brown tape
#16 stems: 4 18″ pieces, 1 14″ piece
Tape each stem the full length. The short one is the center stem. Twist and spiral the others as illustrated.

Leaves: String dark and light green at random.

Basic 7   Pointed top   [34]
Rows 11   and bottom
Tape the hanging wires of leaves.

Assembly:

a. Anchor and tape leaves to branches as illustrated with 1½″ of leaf stem showing.
b. Fruit or flowers may be added to branches. For "partridge in a pear tree" add one partridge and hang 5 pears on to tree.

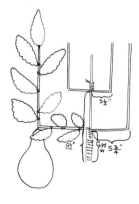

MING TREE of Mugho Pine

Materials

#34 lacing wire for tree
Dark and light green beads
Brown or yellow tape *
Manzanita branch or a piece of driftwood
*If "sandblasted" manzanita is used, use the yellow tape.

30 clusters will produce a medium-sized tree. Each cluster consists of: 16 *single beaded units in dark green. 10 *single beaded units in light green
Each unit measures 1⅛" of beads.
*Advanced procedures, single beaded units, Method I.
Start and end with 3" of bare wire.

Assembly of Clusters:

a. Arrange the 10 units of light green together and surround them with the 16 units of dark green.
b. Join all pieces of the cluster evenly and twist the hanging wires 2 or 3 times at the base of the beads.

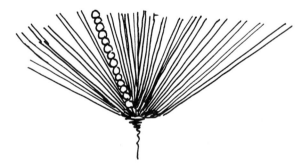

c. Thin out the hanging wires so they are not too bulky.
d. Tape the hanging wires.

Assembly of Clusters on to Manzanita:

METHOD I: Tape the clusters to the manzanita branch, spacing them attractively. Paint the tape *and* manzanita with shoe dye. (Use brown dye for regular, beige for sandblasted.)

METHOD II: After taping each cluster, you can cover the tape with clay and cover the clay with sheet moss.

Assembly of Clusters on to Driftwood:

a. Drill a hole in the driftwood wherever you wish to place a cluster.
b. Glue the cluster into the hole. (You may have to shorten hanging stems for this method.)
c. Place clay around the opening of the hole and cover clay with sheet moss, lichen, or birch shavings.

Planting:

The tree may be planted in a container with plaster of Paris.
Bring the plaster to the consistency recommended on the box and let stand for about twenty minutes in the container you are using. Place the base of the tree in the plaster and support it until the plaster sets.
When the plaster is thoroughly dry, mix some glue with an equal part of water to thin it. Spread it over the plaster. Sprinkle with colored-glass "fish chips," which may be purchased in a pet shop. Green or black look best.

ORIENTAL BLOSSOM TREE

Materials

#25 gold wire or #28 silver wire
Any warm color plus black for the centers
Crystal or cut crystal may be used
Brown tape
Manzanita branch or driftwood

The count given is for 1 spray of 3 bud units—
3 flowers make as many sprays as needed for
the size of the manzanita branch or driftwood
you are working with.
Leave very long bottom basic loops on all
units, as the entire spray is assembled on its
own hanging stems.

Buds: Triple split basic

Unit 1	Basic 4	Round top	[1]
			per spray
	Rows 5	and bottom	
Unit 2	Basic 4	As above	[2]
	Rows 7		
Flower:	Basic 4	Round top	[5]
			per spray
	Rows 7	and bottom	
	Make three flowers.		

Centers: 3—12-bead loops, all on one wire
[1 per flower]
Keep loops very round.

Assembly of Flower:

a. Joint the hanging stems of the flower petals and twist three times.
b. Fan out petals so fronts face up.
c. Add the center and twist once more. Cut away bottom basic loops.
d. Tape the hanging stems of all flowers and buds.
e. Buds are assembled the same way with fronts facing out.

Assembly of Spray:

a. Tape one unit under another in the following order:

Smallest bud at top	1 flower 1½" below
1 large bud ½" below	1 flower 1½" below
1 large bud ¾" below	1 flower 2" below

b. Each spray is taped on to the manzanita
or glued into the holes of the driftwood, as
described for Ming tree.

At the *base* of the bush, gracefully place
around 3 or 4 of the following larger flowers:

Petals:	Basic 4	Round top	[5]
	Rows 11	and bottom	
Domed Center:	Basic 4	Keep round	[1]
	Rows 10		
Leaves:	Basic ¾"	Pointed top	[4]
	Rows 5	Round bottom	

Assembly:

a. Twist together hanging wires of the 5 petals.
b. Fan out so all petal fronts face up.
c. Straddle domed center across flower.
d. Twist all wires once more. Cut away bottom basic loops.
e. Tape hanging stems.
f. Tape leaves 1" under flower, spacing evenly around.
g. Tape remainder of stem.

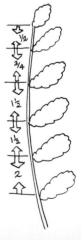

PALM TREE

Materials

#26 and #30 silver wire
Dark green beads
Brown tape
#16 stem wires
Drinking straw
String 40″ of beads on to the #30 wire.
String 3″ on to the #26 wire.

Fronds:

The base will show a "seam" running down the center when completed.

a. Twist the ends of both wires together five times.

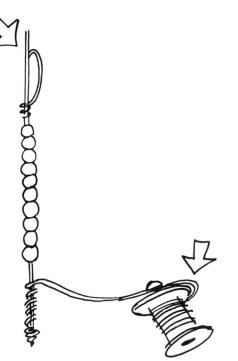

b. Cut away the spool of #26 wire, leaving 3″ of bare wire.

c. Form the bare wire into a loop, twisting firmly against the beads, to hold them taut. This becomes the base, and the twist will be opened later.

d. With the beads on #30 wire, make a 2″ horizontal loop on each side of the base. Complete a full 1½ turns, just like a *basic* turn.

e. Make another 2″ loop on each side of the base, working the basic turn between the

third and fourth bead down the base. This leaves 2 beads between each set of loops.

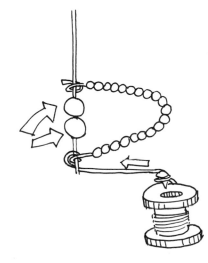

f. Repeat *e* until 10 loops are on each side of the base. [8]

Repeat entire process with 7 loops on each side of the base. [4]

157

Assembly of Fronds:

a. On each frond, trim the twist where the 2 wires were secured together.

b. Bend them back as a basic.

c. Open the 3″ bare-wire loop and twist 2 fronds together as a unit. Beads remaining on the base become the stem of the frond.

d. Narrow all loops and angle them up toward the top.

Assembly of Tree:

a. Tape 2 full lengths of stem wire. Tape the 2 together.

b. Set them into a straw and tape the straw to the stem wire.

c. Reinforce the bottom of the straw with added tape.

d. Tape a short frond to the top on one side of the stem with the "seam" facing the stem.

e. Tape another short frond just opposite in the same manner.

f. Tape the longer fronds under this to fit evenly around the stem.

g. Be sure to pull down on the bare-wire stems as you tape to secure the frond tightly against the stem.

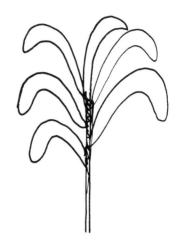

SUGAR PLUM TREE

Materials

#28 silver wire
Speckled chalk in any color
Dark green for calyx
Dark green tape

Sugar Plum: 4–1″ loops, all on one wire; oval loops [15 per plum]
Seventeen plums per tree
Leave 8″ stems at the beginning and end of each set of loops. These become the trunk of the tree.

Calyx: 8–2″ loops, all on one wire; oval loops [1 per plum]

Procedure: Measure 8″ of bare wire. At this point measure 1″ of beads. Form into a loop and twist twice just below beads. Continue to make 1″ loops, right next to each other, twisting twice below each loop. End with 8″ of bare wire. Cut away from spool.

Assembly of Plums:

a. Divide the 15 units into 3 equal parts.

b. Twist *each part* together under the beads.

c. Slide one part over another.

d. Twist all parts securely for ½″ below the beads.

e. Tape for ½″.

f. Place calyx under the plum and tape down entire stem. The end result will be 3 layers high. All loops stand on end.

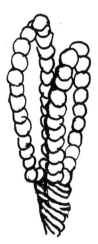

Assembly of Tree:

a. Using 1 sugar plum as the top of the tree and the hanging wires as the "trunk," add a second plum 1½″ below the first.

b. Tape the stem of the second plum to the "trunk" with 1″ of its own stem extending away from the trunk.

c. Add 2 more plums evenly around the trunk at the same level, taping them on one at a time. Each time you add a new plum, be sure to tape all the way down the trunk.

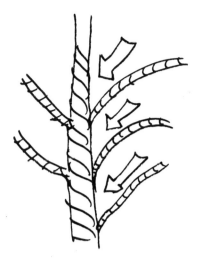

d. Add the next 3 plums one at a time, 1½″ below, in the open spaces left by the upper 3. On these 3 have each plum extending away from the trunk 1¼″.

e. Continue in this manner, dropping down 1½″ for each 3 plums.

f. Every time you add a new group, extend branch ¼″ farther away from trunk.

The last level has 4 plums instead of 3.

Shaping of Plums:

Each oval loop is separated from another. Pull them in every direction, making sure they stand on their sides instead of lying flat.

Planting:

The last row of plums stands about 2″ above the top of the pot.

a. The pot for the tree should measure 4″ in diameter. Fill it with 2″ of clay.

b. Spread out the bottom branches so they look like roots of a tree. Press them into the clay. (Spreading the branches gives better leverage to the tree.)

c. Fill the rest of the pot with clay to within ½″ of the top.

d. Cover the clay with sheet moss.

9

Boutique

The uniqueness of boutique pieces offers new dimensions in beading. Each item is stimulating to work on and will provide tremendous enjoyment.

May we offer a few suggestions?

Fill the woven basket with nuts or mints and use it for party decorations.

The spiraled basket can be used as an ornamental piece, or filled with small flowers, such as cineraria or strawflowers.

The bumblebee, butterfly, dragonfly, or peacock looks lovely when added to any arrangement as an accessory.

The partridge and a few beaded pears, when added to the espalier tree, will make "a partridge in a pear tree."

The tortoiseshell mirror can be used on a table or hung on a wall.

The poodle, which will be adored by children and adults alike, looks best when planted in a mug or a narrow-necked bottle.

BASKET, SPIRALED

Materials
#26 silver wire for spiraling
#32 binding wire
Three shades of any color crystal
Tape color to match bead color closely
Cardboard shape, 3¼" x 5"

Entire basket is made of varying lengths of a three-strand spiral.

Procedure for Spirals:
String the required length of beads for one shade. Knot the end of the wire. Let all beads slide down to the knot. Cut the wire free from the spool, leaving 2" of bare wire. Knot the cut end. Repeat with each of the other 2 shades. Twist all three starting wires together for ½". Twist all three ending wires together. Hold all 3 strands of beads together and spiral them. Keep the colors in order.
It is easier to use 3 separate spools, if you have them. String each color on a separate spool. Spiral the amounts needed and proceed as instructed.

Spirals: 8½": Bottom outside brace
               15" and 17": Top braces
               25": Handle
               160": Body of basket

Bottom Inside Brace:
Cut three 8" lengths of #26 wire. Twist together for entire length and tape.

Top Braces:
(15" and 17" spirals)
a. Close each spiral into a circle by twisting the end wires tightly.
b. Trim and bend back against beads.

Handle:
(25" spiral)
a. Form the spiral into a circle and close like the top braces.
b. Fold in half and spiral both halves together.

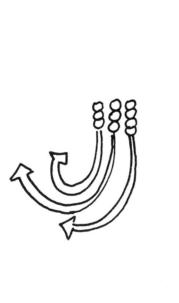

Body of Basket:
(160″ spiral)

a. Hold the beginning parallel with the bottom of the cardboard shape.

b. Wrap the entire unit around the height of the cardboard, keeping each row next to another.

c. Withdraw the cardboard and set the unit on a table. Press all the U-turns in one direction.

Assembly of Basket:

a. Hold the first U-turn of the body on top of the bottom inside brace, ¼″ from the tip of the brace.

b. Place the bottom outside brace (8½″ spiral) on top of *a*.

c. Using a 3″ piece of binding wire, tie all 3 together with 5 tight turns of the wire.

d. Trim away all but ⅛″ of the binding wire and press to inside of taped base.

e. Set the next U-turn closely against the first one and bind in place.

f. Continue to hold each succeeding U-turn close to the previous one and bind in position. End at the bottom of the last U.

g. Form the basket into an oval with the bottom inside brace on the inside, the bottom outside brace on the outside, and the body of the basket sandwiched in between. Twist the ends of the inside brace tightly and trim away all but ¼″.

h. Twist the open ends of the body together tightly. Trim wire and press to the inside. Do the same for the bottom *outside* brace.

i. Set the 15″ top brace on the outside of the basket 1″ down from the top.

j. With a 3″ piece of binding wire, bind the brace to the right-hand side of one U-turn.

k. Bind the brace in four equal distances around to hold it in position.

l. Trim all binding wires and press to inside.

m. Bind each U around basket on right side of U. Leave ⅛″ between each upright row. Trim binding wires. Tuck to inside.

n. Set the 17″ top brace over the basket ½″ down from the top.

o. Bind on the *left* side of each U, as in k, l, m.

p. Hold one end of the handle over the lower top brace at the center point of the basket and bind in place. Bind again near the top.

q. Repeat for the opposite side of the handle.

BASKET, WOVEN

Materials

#32 silver or #28 gold wire for stringing beads
Any color beads in cut crystal
White tape
#18 stem wire: 2—18″ pieces, 5—9″ pieces

Procedure:

a. Tape all stems.
b. Tape 4 short ones together side by side at center point (Unit #1).
c. Tape 1 short stem between 2 long stems side by side at center point (Unit #2).
d. Place the 2 sections over each other, like a cross. Tape together at center point.
e. Hold all stems firmly in the center and fan out into a circle.
f. String one full double bunch of beads on to wire. Anchor open end of wire to the center point of the circle.
g. Starting with Unit #2, push the beads gently toward the frame.

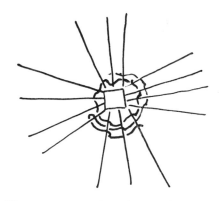

h. Weave over and under each stem, all the way around to the starting point.

i. Weave in the next stem and turn back.

163

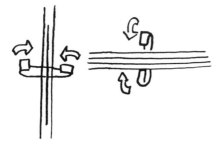

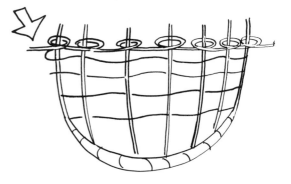

o. Cut the stem ends of Unit #1 ½″ above the final row. *Do not cut Unit #2.*

p. Using pliers, turn the ends to the inside of the basket.

q. Weave the 3 stems of Unit 2 for ¾″.

r. Cut the center stem and turn it to the inside of the basket.

j. Weave again in the same manner until you reach the first turn made. Weave the next stem and turn back.

k. Continue weaving back and forth until the bottom measures 2″ in diameter.

l. Hold the beads and frame firmly and turn each stem upright to form the sides of the basket.

m. Continue to weave the sides until basket measures 1½″ high. End at starting point.

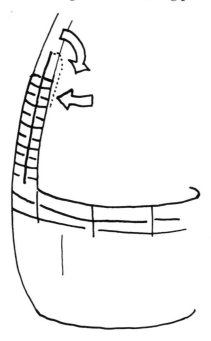

n. On the next row, make a complete turn around *each* stem, as you weave back to the starting point.

s. Wrap beads around the 2 long stems for ½″, drawing them together as you wrap. Cut away from spool and anchor wire with 2 turns around the stems.

t. Anchor the feed wire to the opposite side of Unit #2 and repeat the weaving as in q and r.

u. Continue to wrap the long stems together for ½″, drawing them together.

v. Bend the long wires into a hairpin shape, overlapping them by 2″. (This becomes the handle of the basket.) Tape the exposed wires together. Cut off any excess wire that overlaps.

w. With the beads still on the feed wire, cut away from spool, leaving 8″ of bare wire. Knot the end.

x. Jewel the handle, going over and around it with the free end.

y. Cut away excess and twist with the wire that is anchored on the opposite side.

z. Trim the twist and obscure it within the beads.

BUMBLEBEE

Materials
#25 and #28 gold wire
Yellow and black chalk for the body
2 white beads for the eyes
Yellow tape
#18 stem wire, 2″ long
1½″ piece of drinking straw

Two Wings: Yellow on #25 wire
    Basic 5   Round top
    Rows 5   Pointed bottom

Body:
a. Insert stem wire through the straw, even with the top. Tape in place.
b. String 6″ of black on the #28 wire.
c. String 7″ of yellow on the #25 wire, then add 1 white bead, 2 black, 1 white, and 1″ of black. Cut from spool, leaving 2″ of bare wire.
d. Leave 1″ of bare wire and loop the 2⅛″ of black, which includes the 2 white beads.

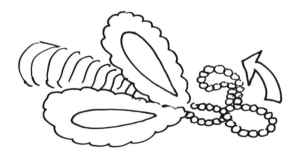

e. Leave 1″ of bare wire and anchor the #25 wire around the base of the black loop.
f. Knot the end of both wires to hold beads in place.

g. Hold the black loop to the top of the straw with the bare wires running down the straw. Tape these wires to the body.
h. Twist the black loop into a figure eight, fold in half, and press the top half up through the bottom half of the eight to form the head.
i. Hold both colors tightly against the body next to each other and jewel the body.
j. Twist ends around the lower edge of body and tape.
k. hold one wing to one side of the upper part of the .body, just below the head. Twist the bare wire completely around the body and end it on the underside for a leg.
l. Repeat with the second wing opposite the first.

BUTTERFLY

Materials

#25 gold wire
Any color or a variety of colors in crystal
White tape
Gold wax stain (Treasure Gold or Rub 'n' Buff)
Small bar pin

Wings:

SMALLER WINGS: Make 2.
   Basic ¼″   Pointed top
   Rows 5   Round bottom

LARGER WINGS: Make 2.
   Basic ¼″   As above
   Rows 7

Make each butterfly with a left set of wings and a right set of wings. This is accomplished by curving the top basic wire, as you work, in the direction you wish the wing to curve.

Body: 1–1″ loop wrapped once

Antennae: ¾″ of beads for each one. Make 2.
            Single beaded stems, Method II.

Assembly:

a. Join each pair of wings by twisting the hanging wires directly below the beads.

b. Join the two pairs together so tips face out and smaller wings are above and back of larger wings.
c. Thin out hanging wires.
d. Join body and antennae together by twisting hanging wires close under beads.
e. Set this unit on top of wings with body to the rear and antennae facing the front. Twist all hanging wires together 3 or 4 times.
f. Thin out hanging wires once more and tape them.
g. Attach hanging wire to a pin with the very finest wire.
h. Cover exposed wire with tape.

Butterfly may be used for the following:
Flower arrangements: Just tape to a stem wire or set on top of flower.
Candle decoration: Twist all hanging wires firmly, all the way down.
Do not tape wires. Hold butterfly in tweezers or tongs and heat over a flame. Immediately insert into candle.
Hair ornament: Attach to a bobby pin or hair clip with finest wire.
Hors d'oeuvres picks: Attach to a plastic pick with gold lacing wire.

DRAGONFLY

Materials
#25 gold wire
Any vivid color plus black in crystal
White tape
#18 stem wire, 3″ long

String black and color at random, ending with 10 black beads.

Head:
Start with 1″ of bare wire, then make 2–5-bead loops next to each other. Spiral 1″ of bare wire together with the starting 1″. Do not cut away from spool. Using the spiraled wire as a top basic, push 3 beads to within ½″ of the top basic. Make a bottom basic loop and work for 7 rows. Keep the petal round. End as usual.

Upper Wings:	Basic 12	Round top	[2]
	Rows 9	Semipointed bottom	
Lower Wings:	Basic 6	As above	[2]
	Rows 11		

Assembly:
a. Cut away bottom basic loops.
b. Twist the 2 upper wings together in an east-west position.
c. Twist the 2 lower wings together the same way.
d. Tape the hanging wires of the head to the #18 stem wire.
e. Tape the hanging wires of the wings to the stem wire.
f. Jewel the stem in the solid vivid color. This becomes the body.
g. End the jeweling by winding the wire just under the beads and cut away, leaving ½″ of bare wire.
h. Spiral this bare wire around a needle. Single beaded stems, Method II

EPERGNE OF FRUITS AND FLOWERS

Materials

One pie plate, 8″ in diameter
One 4½″ metal funnel
Two 4″ metal funnels
One 18″ piece of ⅜″ dowel
Five empty wire spools (with at least a ⅜″ center hole)
One block of shelving board, 4″ x 4″
Spray paint of any desired color
Five screws
Felt to cover bottom of pie plate
Clay

Procedure:

a. Mark the center of the pie plate and the center of the block of wood.
b. Drill a ⅜″ hole through the wood only. Set in the dowel.
c. Use the center mark of the plate and screw the block to the inside, working from the bottom up. Screw the 4 corners of the block. Countersink the screws.
d. Glue a piece of felt to the bottom.
e. Set the large funnel onto the dowel, wide side up.

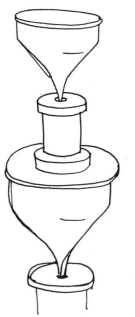

f. Add: 2 spools, 1 small funnel, 2 spools, 1 small funnel, and 1 spool.
g. Spray-paint and allow to dry overnight.

Fillers for Funnels:

TOP FUNNEL: Set clay around the base to hold the following:
3 sprays of autumn leaves to hang down the sides
2 sprays of salvia or any other light airy flowers

CENTER FUNNEL: No clay is needed; just set in the following fruits:
2 kumquats; 1 lemon; 1 plum; 1 bunch of grapes to hang down

LOWER FUNNEL: No clay is needed; set in the following fruits:
1 orange; 1 pear; 2 bananas

Plate:

Cover the block of wood with a mound of clay:
1 wood rose with a 2″ stem on one side
1 tulip tree flower with a 3″ stem and 2 small leaves on the opposite side
4 strawflowers set in each corner
2 grape bunches of different colors to be draped between

MIRROR,
TORTOISESHELL

Materials

#28 gold wire for berries and sewing
#25 gold wire for leaves
One oval of ¼″ hardware mesh
One oval of mirror plus cardboard pattern,
17″ x 13″
One oval of Masonite
Mirror glue
Cloth gummed tape
4 double bunches of tortoiseshell beads
Brown beads for trim
Gold beads for berries
A large darning needle to sew

Leaves: Basic 1½″   Pointed top   [85]
Rows 9   and bottom
Work the first 7 rows in tortoiseshell.
Estimate enough wire to complete 2
more rows, and cut wire free from
spool. String brown on to wire and
complete petal.

Berries:

Basic 4   Deep dome petal [20]
Rows 12
Work the last 4 rows very tightly to
close berry. Twist and spiral the end
wires for stems.

Assembly:

a. Cover the edge of the wire mesh with
cloth gummed tape. Press it down on one
side and then turn over the edge.

b. Staple the pattern of the mirror onto the mesh, centering properly, to allow a margin for wiring on the leaves.

c. Start at the top and wire and sew the leaves as illustrated.

d. Cluster 5 berries, set them through the mesh in the proper place, with 1″ of stem showing. Remove the pattern of the mirror.

e. Punch 2 holes near the top third of the Masonite. Slip heavy wire through the holes to hang the mirror.

f. Staple the Masonite to the back of the mesh.

g. Glue the mirror to the front. Place a heavy book on top and allow to dry over night.

h. Arrange the leaves to cover all the mesh.

PARTRIDGE

Materials
#24 or #25 gold wire
Black, topaz, and brown in crystal

Body: String brown, black and topaz at random.
Do not cut any basic wires.
Basic ¾″   Round top   [2]
Rows 17   Pointed bottom
After seventh row, reduce the round top by 1 bead each row for the remainder of the petal.

Head: Black
Do not cut any basic wires.
Basic 5   Pointed top   [2]
Rows 7   Round bottom
After fourth row, reduce the round bottom by 1 bead each row for the remainder of the petal.

Top Wings: String 2″ each of black, topaz, and brown. Leave 4″ of bare wire, then make 3—2″ loops, all on one wire.

Bottom Wings: String 3″ each of black, topaz, and brown, and repeat again for 3″ of each. Leave 4″ of bare wire, then make 6—3″ loops, all on one wire.

Assembly:
a. Hold the body petals together, front sides out, and twist the top and bottom basic wires.

b. Hold the head petals together at the point. Twist the basic wires, and set them to the inside. Bring the petals together and twist the end wires.

c. Bring the top wing end wires together and twist with the head end wires. Twist this together with the top body wire. *Note:* This wire may be used to assemble the partridge to the pear tree, so do not cut.

d. Bring the bottom wing end wires together and twist to the bottom body wire. Same note as above.

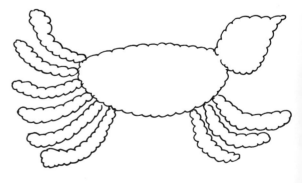

PEACOCK

Materials

#28 gold wire for the eyes on the tail
#25 gold wire for the body
Royal blue for the bird
Turquoise for the tail feathers
Yellow for the eyes on the tail
Yellow tape

Body: Use a 3″ top basic wire and a 5″ bottom basic loop.
Do not cut basic wires.

Basic ¾″	Round top	[2]
Rows 15	Pointed bottom	

After the seventh row, reduce the round top by 1 bead on each row.

Head: Use a 5″ bottom basic loop.
Do not cut basic wires.

Basic 6	Semipointed top	[2]
Rows 7	Round bottom	

After the third row, reduce the round bottom by 1 bead on each row. Cut the ending wire even with the bottom basic loop.

Tail Feathers:

Basic 1½″	Semipointed top	[6]
Rows 7	and bottom	

Eyes on Tail:

String a few inches of yellow. For each eye add 6 royal-blue beads. Make a 6-bead loop, wrapped once. Twist end wires twice. Bring one end to the opposite side of the circle. Draw it over and down again, across the yellow loop.   [6]

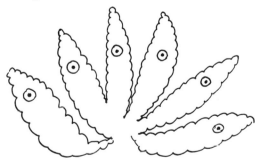

Assembly:

a. Set the body petals together side by side. Twist the top basic wires only twice, ending on the outside.

b. Twist all wires of the loops together and tape down for the tail.

c. Set the head petals together, twist the top basic wires, and draw them between the two petals to meet the bottom basic loops.

d. Open the loops at the bottom, thus having six wires together.

e. Wind one wire around all six to bring them together just under the head. Wind only twice.

f. String ¾″ of royal beads on to each wire. Twist 2 together to lock the beads in place.

g. Spiral these beaded wires together for the throat.

h. Twist the bare-wire ends around the top basic wires of the body.

i. Set this bare wire under the body, inside the two petals.

j. Wire the tail eyes to the tail just on top of the first row.

k. Twist three feathers together at the hanging wires. Tape the wires.

l. Repeat with 3 more feathers. Bend the taped end at right angles.

m. Hold one set of feathers at the pointed end of the body, beads touching beads, on one side, and tape to the tail of the body.

171

n. Repeat this with the second set of feathers, next to the first set. (Fan out from one side, across the top, to the opposite side.)

o. Cut 2–6" pieces of #25 gold wire. Slip them, one at a time, through the underside of the body close to the front end. Use one row of each petal and catch the twisted wires of the throat.

p. Center these wires and twist 2 together for ¾", one on each side of the body.

q. Use the remaining ends of the "leg" wires. Bend them in half, and then in half again, for "claws" of the bird.

r. Set the legs and the tail so they hold the bird upright.

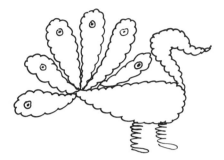

PICTURE FRAME, VICTORIAN

Materials

Ball of wrapping twine
#1 crochet hook
2 yards of clothesline rope
Flour and water to make a paste
Copal varnish
Gilt
Nylon netting to cover the stitches at back of the frame
Tortoiseshell beads in crystal
Brown and gold beads in crystal
#25 and #28 gold wire
11" x 15" oval frame
Deep tray large enough to hold frame flat for stiffening process
Darning needle and nylon thread

Leaves: Tortoiseshell on #25 gold wire
            Basic 1½"   Pointed top   [76]
            Rows 9   and bottom

Complete 7 rows. Cut away enough bare wire to finish 2 more rows. String brown on and complete the petal.

Berries: Gold beads on #28 gold wire
            Basic 4   Dome petal   [20]
            Rows 12

Work the last 4 rows very tightly to close the berries.

Assembly:

a. Sew the leaves and berries in place as illustrated.

b. Cut the netting on a bias. Sew to the back of the frame to cover the stitching.

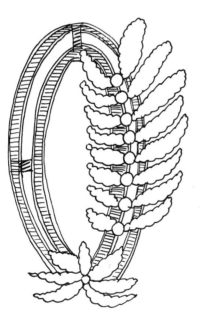

Crocheting of Frame:

Cast on 280 stitches. Judge the size of an oval to meet the requirements. If correct, close the loop with a slip stitch, and continue around:

Row 1: Work a short double crochet (SDC) in each stitch around. Mark the top and bottom with a piece of black thread.

Row 2: Work SDC going through both veins of the stitches. Widen this row by working 2 SDC in one stitch in each of 10 stitches, at the bottom and top of oval.

The remainder of the stitches will be increased with 2 SDC in every tenth stitch.

Row 3: Same as the second row, but do the increasing at the 2 side portions of the oval.

Row 4: SDC in each stitch around.

Row 5: SDC in each stitch and increase in every fifteenth stitch.

Row 6: Same as Row 5, but increase in every sixteenth stitch.

Row 7: Same as Row 5, but increase in every seventeenth stitch.

Row 8: Hold the rope on the frame, and work single crochet stitches around it, in every stitch.

Start a separate strip. Cast on 440 stitches. This becomes a second oval, to fit around the first, and will be attached with small bands. This oval is 2" larger than the first. Judge the size before continuing.

Join in a ring and work 4 rows with SDC. Increase the first row with 2 SDC in every tenth stitch; increase the second row in every eleventh stitch, and so on. Be sure it is flat. Make 4 bands of 12 stitches and 5 rows. Sew these bands to the top, bottom, and 2 sides, connecting both pieces as illustrated.

Finishing:

In the tray mix enough paste to cover this. Soak the frame, set it on waxed paper to dry. Repeat this two more times. When stiff and dry, give it two coats of varnish. Allow to dry between coats. When dry, mix a little gilt with the varnish and give it a final coat.

POODLE

Materials

#28 silver wire
#32 binding wire
White or light gray crystal
Black for eyes and nose
Red for tongue
White tape
#16 stem wire

Unit 1:	5–1¼″ loops, all on one wire		[12]
Unit 2:	5–1½″ loops, all on one wire		[16]
Unit 3:	7–1¾″ loops, all on one wire		[12]
Unit 4:	7–2″ loops, all on one wire		[12]
Black:	Basic 4 Rows 5	Round top Pointed bottom	[3]
Red:	Basic ¾″ Rows 7	Round top Pointed bottom	[1]

Assembly:

a. Cluster 3 of Unit 1 together and twist bare wires.

b. Bind on 4 of Unit 2, to fit evenly around. Use the hanging wires of a as a stem.

c. Bind on 3 of Unit 3, spacing evenly around, just under b.

d. Bind on 3 of Unit 4, as above.

e. Tape all hanging wires.

f. Repeat this entire procedure from a to e 3 more times.

g. Use 1 cluster as the head and tape to a 12″ piece of stem wire.

h. Tape one cluster on each side just below the head. Face them east and west.

i. Tape on the final cluster just below the two. Bring it forward a little and divide the *lower half* in two, facing them away from each other.

j. Push the eyes and nose into the clusters as illustrated.

k. Push the tongue through just where the bottom cluster divides.

l. Add the bow to the top of the head.

m. Tape all wires and place poodle into a narrow-necked container.

Bows for Poodle:

a. Lay a piece of bare wire along the length of a pencil.

b. Wind beaded spool wire around both. Keep rows close together.

c. When the necessary number of coils (thirty) are completed, slip them off the pencil along with the bare wire.

d. Join both ends of the coiled wire.

e. Cut away spool wire.

f. Hold both ends of the single piece of bare wire and pull tightly to close up circle.

g. Twist securely and cut away excess wire.

h. Grasp center coil and gently pull away from rest of coils, forming a horizontal V.

This is half of the bow. Repeat the entire process and join the 2 halves together.

To make a ruff for the poodle's neck, use the same procedure, but use a very thick piece of wood dowel instead of a pencil.

"STITCH IN TIME"

Materials

#28 and #25 gold wire
Assorted colors of beads in crystal for minia-
ture bouquets
White and gold beads in crystal
Light and dark green
Brown tape
1″ thickness of Styrofoam
2 pieces of black felt to cover form
Colored-head straight pins
4 large red sequins
8 threaded needles (optional)
Glue
#20 stem wire

Clock Form:

Cut the Styrofoam to form and cover with
felt, gluing in place.

Miniature Bouquets: Any color on #28 gold
wire   [18]
a. Make 6–8-bead loops, all on one wire.
b. Cut from spool, leaving 3″of bare wire.
c. String 8 beads of a complementary color
on the bare wire.
d. Form these into a loop. Set in center with
the 6 loops surrounding the single loop.
e. Twist end wires firmly for a stem.
f. Make 18 different colors.

Foliage for Bouquets: Light green on #28
gold wire
a. Leave 2″ of bare wire and make a 6-bead
loop.
b. Spiral the end wires 7 times and make
another 6-bead loop on one side of the spiral.
c. Spiral the end wires again, down the stem
7 times, and repeat loop on opposite side.
d. Repeat until 6 loops are made.   [11]
e. Make 1 leaf with only 4 loops.   [1]

Face of Clock: White on #25 gold wire
a. Working only with bare wire, allow a 3″
top basic and make 2–4″ bottom basic loops.
b. Open the loops at the oval edge and fan
these wires out for a round frame.
c. Use each wire for a basic turn, keeping
the frame flat, and fill each space with beads
until it measures 2½″ across. Cut all end
wires and bend back as usual.

Levels for Clock: Dark green on #25 gold wire Work with a 6″ bottom loop.
Basic 1″   Semipointed top   [2]
Rows 11   and bottom
Cut feed wire even with bottom basic loop.

Pendulum: Gold beads on #25 gold wire
Unit 1:   5—10-bead loops, all on one wire
Unit 2:   6—15-bead loops, all on one wire
Unit 3:   12—2″ loops, all on one wire
Unit 4:   8—¾″ loops, all on one wire

Assembly of Bouquets:

a. Twist 3 different colors together as a cluster with 2 units of foliage.
b. One cluster has one short and one long leaf.

Assembly of Clock Face:

a. Wire the red sequins to be at 12, 3, 6, and 9 o'clock.
b. Set the miniature bouquet with the short leaf into the center.
c. Fasten to the back with a small piece of wire. Cluster the flowers close to the center and set the long leaf at 12 o'clock and the short leaf at 3 o'clock.

Assembly of Entire Pincushion:

a. Staple and glue the face to the center of the form.
b. Staple and glue each level at the bottom, 1″ in from the sides.
c. Staple and glue the pendulum to the center of the bottom.
d. Staple and glue 1 bouquet to each corner of the form as illustrated.
e. Set the threaded needles into the felt, on either side of the pendulum, as chains. Decorate with the colored pins as illustrated.

Assembly of Levels:

a. Twist all bare wire stems of each one separately.
b. Tape for 3½″.

Assembly of Pendulum:

a. Cluster Unit 1 together, set Units 2 and 3 around it. Twist the hanging wires.
b. Tape to the top of an 8″ piece of #20 stem wire.
c. Set Unit 4 under this as a calyx and tape down stem.
d. Bend the pendulum at right angles to the stem.

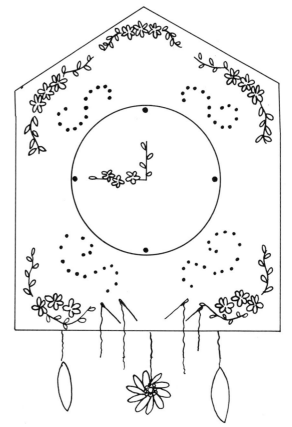

SWITCH-PLATE COVER

Materials

#25 gold wire
Assorted colors of crystal or chalk
Black for centers
Light green tape
Corrugated cardboard

Procedure:

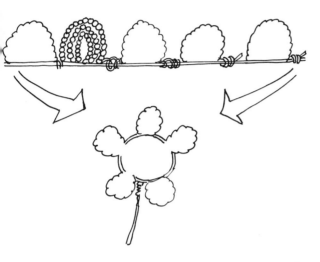

a. With bare wire, use a 2″ top basic, and make a 10″ bottom basic loop.
b. Working toward the long loop end, make a 10-bead loop on one side, making a complete turn around the base.
c. Working back toward the shorter end, make 1 wrap around the 10-bead loop. Make a complete turn around the base.
d. Make a second wrap, going back again toward the long loop. Turn as above.
e. Repeat until 5 petals are completed.
f. Open the loop, cut the feed wire even with the loop.
g. Bring the end wires together to close the petals into a circle.
h. Twist all hanging wires.
i. Make 8 flowers.

Center: With bare wire, use a 2″ top basic and make a 6″ bottom basic loop.
Basic 3   Round top
Rows 10   and bottom
Do not cut away the top basic.

Assembly:

a. Insert the center top basic wires through the first loop of the top petal.
b. Draw this down the back and twist all bare wires together for the stem.
c. Tape the stem for 4 to 6 inches. Vary the lengths of the flowers.
d. Use the illustrated pattern and cut corrugated cardboard with the grooves running vertically. This may be spray-painted any color. Set the stems into the grooves.

Cut out the center oblong and mark the dots for the plate screws.

Remove only the screws and place this over the metal plate. Set back the screws.

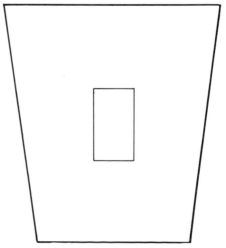

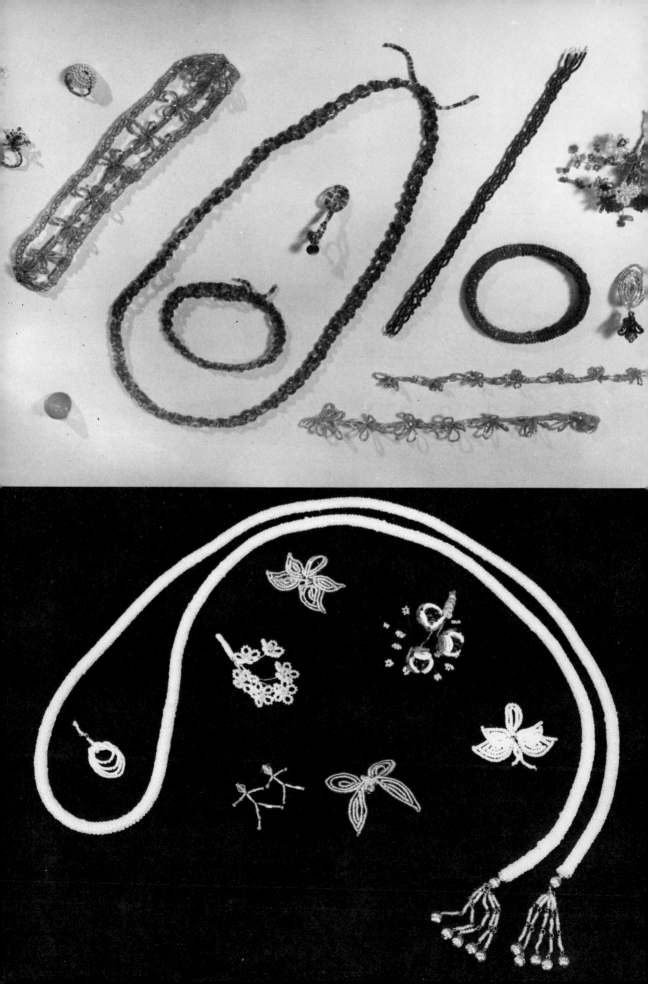

10

Jewelry

Each jewelry design lends itself to delicate elegance or exotic extravaganza, depending entirely upon your use of color. Suit your own taste, and add an interesting and unusual adornment to your wardrobe. Depict the effect you wish to create, work carefully to give your pieces a professional quality, and your ornaments will be a delight to own.

All the designs look particularly smart when made in pearls, gold lined, silver lined, or cut-crystal beads. Try to find unusual clasps.

This different and novel approach to beading should give you hours of enjoyment.

BELT, KNOTTED

Materials

#28 gold wire
Two shades of any color

Procedure:

a. String four times the length desired. Make a 3″ bare-wire loop on the open end of the wire.

b. Send all the beads toward this loop and cut away 3″ of bare wire. Loop this end to lock the beads in place. Repeat this with the second color.

c. Fold both strands in half and straddle over a pencil as illustrated.

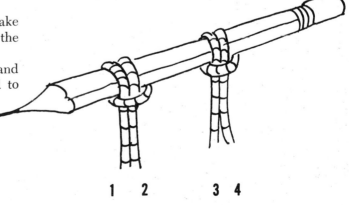

1 2   3 4

d. Make the knots in the following manner:

e. Make a hairpin fold of String 1. Bring String 2 over the loop and up behind it. Cross over itself and down through the loop.

f. Knot 2 and 3 at 1″ down.

g. Knot 1 and 2 at 1″ under the first knot.

h. Knot 3 and 4 at the same level.

i. Repeat this for the desired length, leaving 3½″ without knots.

j. Open the bare-wire loops of one color and twist tightly together, close to beads. (The ends need not be equal.) Repeat this with the second color. Trim the twist.

k. Spiral both colors together and hide the wire twists in the beads.

l. Slip top loops off the pencil. The spiral end is strung through these loops to close the belt.

BELT, ROPE—Method I

Materials

#34 silver or #32 gold wire, whichever matches the beads most closely

#25 gold wire

Gold, silver, or any desired color in crystal

18 large (8 mm.) beads to match

#4½ clothesline rope (⁹⁄₆₄ diameter)

2 cup-ends (jewelry findings)

Darning needle

Belt: Cut the rope to the desired length (waistline plus 20″ usually).

a. String one full 400″ bunch on to wire.

b. Bind the beginning bare wire 5 times around one end of the rope.

c. Jewel the entire length of the rope.

d. End by binding bare wire 5 times around the end of the rope.

Tassels: Make 6 for each end of the belt.

a. Cut 3–4″ pieces of #25 gold wire.

b. On one piece, string 6 small beads and form a loop at one end.

c. Spiral the bare wires tightly together for ½″.

d. String on 1 large bead and 5 small beads.

e. Hold the wire close to the final bead with pliers. Form a loop of bare wire around the pliers and twist twice around the tassel wire. Trim as illustrated.

f. String 3 small beads on a second piece of wire.

g. Draw an end through the final bare-wire loop of the first unit.

h. Add 3 small beads and form a 6-bead loop. Repeat c, d, and e.

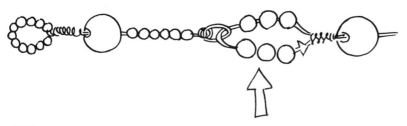

i. Make 1 more section, but end with 3 small beads and 3″ of bare wire.

j. Make 6–3-section units and twist 3 together at the 3-bead end, for a tassel.

Assembly of Tassels to Belt:
a. Wire the tassel to the loop of a cup-end. Trim.

b. Thread a 12″ piece of jeweling wire through the darning needle.
c. Bind an end around the final 1″ of jeweling.
d. Draw the needle through the open end of the cup, around the loop, and back again. Set the rope end tightly into the cup and press the cup sides into the rope.

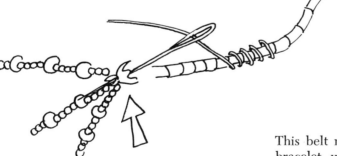

e. Bind once more around 1″ of jeweling. Trim.
f. Repeat on the opposite end of the rope.

This belt may be used for a necklace and a bracelet, with rope cut to proper size. For a necklace shorten the length and make the tassels a little longer. The bracelet will need a ring lock at one end and a jump ring at the other end.

BELT, ROPE—Method II

Materials

#34 lacing wire
One 400″ bunch of any color crystal
Cotton cording (waist measurement plus 24″)
Large-eye needle
Findings (cup-ends and jump rings)
End pins may be made with spool wire. If so, use #26 silver or #25 gold.

Procedure:

a. String a full bunch of beads on to the #34 wire. Leave a long piece of bare wire at the beginning of the spool.
b. Thread the open end of the wire through a needle. Insert through the end of the cord and draw through the cord.
c. Insert the needle through a cup-end, remove the needle, and string on 3 beads.
d. Bring the wire back through the beads, omitting the first bead. Single beaded stem, Method I.
e. Push wire back through cup-end, rethread into needle, and sew through end of cording once more. Wrap around cording several times securely, and cut away the end.
f. Jewel the cording with beads on the spool, for the entire length, securing to cord with a needle and thread every few rows.
g. End like beginning: a, b, c, d, e.

Tassels:

a. Put one end pin through a bead. Make a tight loop on open end. Form a tiny loop on #26 wire. Hook into loop of end pin and tighten. Push up 5 beads, form a tight loop.
b. Continue this procedure until 3 units are completed.
c. Make 7 tassels for each side and attach them to a jump ring.
d. Insert jump ring through the beads of the cup-end.

BRACELET, CHAIN LINKS

Materials

#28 gold wire
Cut-crystal beads
Ring locks

Procedure:

a. String 60″ of beads on to the wire.
b. Allow 1″ of bare wire and make a 1″ bead loop.
c. Make 4–½″ loops set close to the first loop. Form into a cross shape.
d. Make a 1″ loop. You should have a unit as illustrated. Cut free.

e. Twist the beginning and end wire firmly on the underside, 5 times. Trim all but 2 turns of the twist and press into the beads.

f. Start the next unit in the following manner: Allow 1″ of bare wire and measure 1″ of beads.

g. String this through the 1″ loop of the pre-vious unit, then form the new loop. Repeat b, c, and d.

h. Repeat e and continue on until enough units are completed to fit as a bracelet.

i. Secure a ring lock to the first and last 1″ loop.

This method may be used for a necklace and an ankle bracelet.

BRACELET, SOLID LINKS

Materials
#25 and #28 gold wires
Cut-crystal beads
Spring lock and jump ring

Band:
a. String 7½″ on to the #25 gold wire.

b. Grip the bare wire with pliers ½″ from the end and form a tiny loop by bringing the end over the pliers. Spiral this end firmly down the wire.

c. Hold the feed wire up and allow the beads to fall to the twist. Keep taut, but not overly tight.

d. Grip the wire as above, ½″ from the final bead. Cut free with 1″ of bare wire and repeat the twist down the wire. Cut off any excess wire.

Links:
a. String 60″ on to the #28 gold wire.

b. Slip the feed wire through the loop of one end of the band. Fold down 1″ and string back 1″ of beads on to both wires.

c. Form a loop of the 1″, and make 4 more 1″ loops, all to be next to the previous loop.

d. Spiral the feed wire down the ½″ twist of the band. Form a 1″ loop on each side of band.

e. Hold the feed wire with 1″ of beads parallel to the band, and work a basic turn of bare wire around the band. Be sure that the wire snaps down between the beads.

f. Make 4–1″ loops to sit on the band in a cross shape.

g. Bring the feed wire to the right side and repeat e and f until 6 cross shapes are formed.

h. Repeat the parallel of beads to the twist, the 1″ loop on each side, the spiral down the twist, and the 5–1″ loops.

i. End by cutting off 1″ of bare wire. String this through the tiny loop of the band and back into 2 beads of the final loop made.

j. Secure a jump ring to one end, a spring lock to the other end.

BRACELET, SOLID ROUND BANGLE

Materials

#32 silver wire
80″ of beads
Yellow tape
#20 stem wire: two 18″ pieces

Procedure:

a. Tape the full length of each stem wire.
b. Bend one stem wire into a 9″ circle. Judge the size by fitting on wrist. Make any necessary adjustments, then continue around the circle with the remainder of wire.
c. Hold this shape as you tape the wires together into a single circle.
d. Set the second stem adjacent to this and tape to the first circle. Continue taping around until both wires are joined together as one.
e. String the 80″ on to the wire and set a thumbtack on the top of the spool.
f. Tape 3″ of the bare end of the wire onto the frame. Send all the beads toward the frame, then allow 3″ of bare wire. Rewind the remainder of wire and secure this point firmly to the tack.
g. The beaded wire is wound on to the spool for ease of handling.
h. Jewel the entire frame, carefully pushing the beads toward the frame as you work.

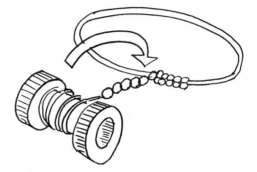

Note: A short length of free wire is necessary all along the beaded wire for a more comfortable turning of the jeweling. If the beads become too taut, open the wire from the tack and allow another inch or two of free wire, then replace the anchoring.
i. At the completion of the jeweling cut off 4″ of bare wire and wind this very firmly around the frame between the rows of beads. Trim any excess.

BRACELET, THREE-STRAND BRAID

Materials

#28 gold wire
Cut-crystal beads
Ring lock and jump ring

Procedure:

a. String 40″ on to the wire.
b. Fold the beginning 2″ of the bare wire. Hold the two sides parallel with a tiny loop at the fold.

c. Push over enough beads to string back on to this 1″ of double wire.
d. Turn the feed wire up and allow 10½″ of beads to fall. This will include the first 1″.
e. Cut free with 4″ of bare wire. Form a fold ½″ from the final bead.
f. Use pliers to help string back into 1″ of beads. Allow a tiny loop to remain above the beads. The string of beads should be taut, but not overly tight.
g. Make 3 as above.
h. Braid these three together, starting ½″ from the edge of the strands.
i. A 3-strand braid is made by holding them side by side. Bring the outer left strand to the

right, over the one next to it, then bring the outer right strand to the left, over the one next to it.
j. Continue to braid until ½″ from the opposite end is reached.
k. Secure a ring lock through the 3 tiny loops of one end and a jump ring through the 3 tiny loops of the other end.

BRACELET, FOUR-STRAND BRAID

Materials

#28 gold wire
Cut-crystal beads
Ring lock and jump ring

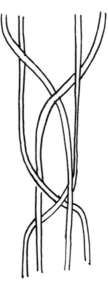

Procedure:

a. Repeat the method of making the strands as described for the three-strand bracelet. Make 4 strands.
b. To make a four-strand braid, hold the 4 ▶ units side by side, at one end.
c. Bring the left strand to the right, over the one next to it.
d. Bring the right strand to the left, under the one next to it and over the next one.

e. Continue to braid, bringing the left strand to the right, over the one next to it. Repeat d. Repeat the assembly instructions of the three-strand bracelet.

BRACELET, THREE SECTIONS

Materials

Same as the three-strand and the solid-link bracelets

Procedure:

a. Make two three-strand bracelets.
b. Start a solid-link bracelet and work 2 cross-shape sections. Work the next one as follows:

c. Make the first 1″ loop to sit on the base.
d. Form the second 1″ loop around the three-strand braid, to lock it into the loop.
e. Make the third 1″ loop to sit on the base, opposite the first.
f. Form the fourth 1″ loop around the alternate three-strand braid.
g. Repeat the solid links as above, except for the final two. These are not anchored around the three-strand braids.
h. Secure a ring lock through all 3 bare-wire loops of one end and a jump ring at the other end.

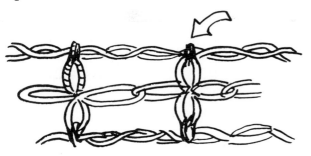

EARRINGS #1

Materials

#32 gold wire
Cut-crystal beads
Pair of half-ball drop ear wires

Procedure:

a. String on 40″ of beads.
b. Allow 2″ of bare wire and form a 1″ loop. Shape into an oval.

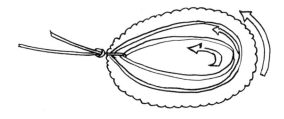

c. Form a 1½″ wrap around this, going around the first free wire as a complete basic turn.
d. Form a 2¼″ wrap around this, as above, keeping the loops flat as you work.
e. Make a 3″ loop around this in the same manner.
f. Cut free with 2″ bare wire.
g. Use the two free wires to secure the loops through the loop of the ear wire.

EARRINGS #2

Materials

#32 gold wire
12″ of any color desired
Pair of drop earrings

Procedure:

a. Thread the starting wire through the loop of the drop and string back into 1½″ of beads.

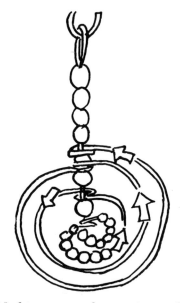

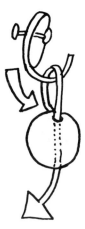

b. Hold this taut to the earring and form a ½″ loop by making a basic turn with the free wire.
c. Wrap twice around this, making the basic turns around one bead above the previous loop made.
d. Match the first 1″ of beads and cut free with 1½″ bare wire.
e. Thread this through the loop of the drop and string back as far as you can.
f. Trim excess wire and spiral the straight lines of the drop.

HAIR-COMB BOW

Silver beads and #28 silver wire

or

Gold beads and #25 gold wire

Triple split unit:

Basic 12   Pointed top
Rows 9   and bottom
Split the basic loop and make 1 petal on each side.
Basic 9   Pointed top
Rows 5   and bottom
Continue with the same feed wire.

Assembly:

a. Make a 1″ loop with 2 loose wraps.
b. Set this to one side.
c. Repeat for the opposite side of the bow, still using the same feed wire.

d. Go over and under the bow between the side petals.

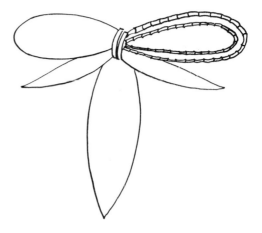

e. Cut free with 3″ of bare wire and use this to secure to a comb or clip.

NECKLACE AND CHAIN BRACELET

Materials

#32 gold wire
Tortoiseshell, gold, or silver is recommended, but any color may be used.

Procedure:

a. String 4½ times the length required.
b. Fold down the first 6″ of starting wire and hold the two wires straight and parallel.
c. Bypass the first bead and allow the rest of the beads to string back on to both wires.
d. Send all the beads down to this end and cut free, leaving 6″ of bare wire.
e. Skip the final bead and string back as far as you can. Pull taut and trim excess wire.

f. Form a ½″ loop, 2″ from one end, by crossing the strands.
g. Hold this loop at the cross in the left hand and feed another loop into this from the underside. Tighten the first loop as though crocheting a chain.
h. Continue to feed loops into the last loop made and tighten the last loop until 2″ of strand remains.
i. String the end through the final loop and pull firmly.
j. Tie a square knot with the ends by sending the right side over the left and around it, then the left side over the right and around it. Pull firmly.

NECKLACE, CHARM

c. String 1″ of beads. Draw the wire through a single bead of one charm at the loop end.

Materials

#28 and #32 gold wires
Any color for the necklace, with an alternate color for the charms
Jump ring and ring lock
The following count is for a 17″ length.

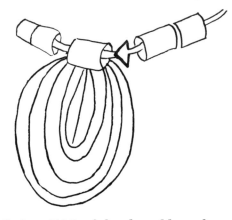

Charms:	Basic 3	Round top	[11]
#28	Rows 5	and bottom	

Work the final twist close to beads, trim and bend back both top and bottom basic wires.

d. String 1½″ of beads, add a charm as above.

e. Continue to add 1½″ of beads and a charm until complete.

Necklace:
#32

a. Cut 26″ of bare wire free from spool.
b. Secure one end to a jump ring.

f. String 1″ of beads and secure the end wire to a ring lock. Trim.

NECKLACE OR BELT, DAISY CHAIN

with pliers. Trim all but ⅛″ and press into back.

b. Hold this unit flat on the table with 2 petals facing up, 2 facing down, and 1 pointing out at each end. This will help you to identify the end loops for assembly.

c. String ⅝″ beads on to the 3″ bare wire of Unit 2.

d. Draw the wire through the center bead of an end loop of Unit 1.

Materials

#28 gold wire
Any color desired for daisy
White pearls for centers

Daisy:		
UNIT 1:	6—1¼″ loops, all on one wire	[1]
UNIT 2:	5—1¼″ loops, all on one wire	[20]

Cut free, leaving 3″ of bare wire.

Centers:	10-bead 3-row crossover	[22]

Use 5 beads for the crossover. Cut free, leaving 1½″ bare wire and end at the top by drawing the wire under and over the center bead of the loop.

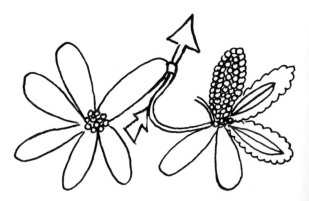

Assembly:

a. Set a center on Unit 1. Bring all wires together at the center underside. Twist firmly

e. Add ⅝" beads to this same wire, draw tight, and complete the final loop of daisy.
f. Set a center on this, and twist and trim like the first unit.
g. Continue as above until all daisies are assembled.
h. To end, make a 2-loop unit. Cut free, leaving 10" bare wire.
i. String ⅝" beads and draw through the center bead of an end loop of the first daisy made.
j. String ⅝" beads and complete the third loop.
k. Make 2 more loops.
l. String ⅝" beads and draw through the center bead of the end loop of the final daisy made.
m. String ⅝" and complete the sixth loop.
n. Set on a center, twist and trim.
This method may be used to make any length desired.

NECKLACE, THREE-STRAND

Materials
#32 gold wire
Stem beads
Any color desired

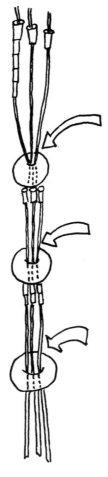

Procedure:
a. Cut 3 pieces of bare wire the desired length, to hang around the neck.
b. Twist the 3 together at one end to anchor the beads. This twist will be opened later.
c. String 10 beads on each wire.
d. String all 3 wires through 1 stem bead.
e. String 10 beads on each wire and repeat d.
f. Repeat c and d until 1½" from end.
g. Open the first twist and use one wire at a time.
h. Go over 1 bead of the opposite end and string through 5 beads. Trim.
i. With second wire, string through 6 beads. Trim.
j. The third wire is strung through 7 beads. Trim.
k. Repeat this with the wires of the opposite end.

PENDANT, HEART

Materials:

Silver beads and #26 silver wire

or

Gold beads and #25 gold wire

Split basic. Start with a 3″ bottom basic loop.
- Basic 5   Pointed top
- Rows 9   Work the bottom as follows:

Procedure:

a. Before you make the first pointed turn, bring the feed wire out to the right for 5 beads.

b. Make a hairpin turn back to the basic wire to form a half of a T.

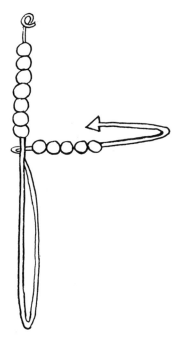

c. Make the pointed turn and repeat this shape on the opposite side.

d. Follow this shape around for the required number of rows.

e. Open the loop close to the beads, twist feed wire up the open loop wire 5 times.

f. String 5 beads on to this new basic wire and repeat the petal as above.

g. Twist the 2 top (pointed) basic wires firmly, trim all but ¼″, and set in between the petals.

h. Close 1″ of the opposite end bare wire into a loop and trim excess.

i. Gently push up on both ends of the T to heart-shape the petals.

PIN, SPRAY

Materials

#28 gold wire
Assorted colors of beads
Medium green
1″ metal pin back

Floret:

a. String 2¾″ of a color, add 8 beads of a compatible color.
b. Allow 3″ of bare wire and form 7–8-bead loops, all on one wire. Cut free, leaving 3″ bare wire.
c. Spiral the 2 end wires firmly down.

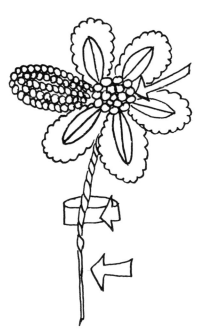

d. Set the 6 loops around the alternate color loop to form a circle. (Make 8 assorted colors.)

Ferns:

a. Allow 4″ of bare wire and make a 6-bead loop.

b. Spiral the feed wire down the bare wire 7 times and form a 6-bead loop close to the spiral.

c. Spiral again down the bare wire 7 times and form a 6-bead loop on the opposite side.
d. Repeat this until 6 loops are complete. Spiral down. [2]
e. Repeat above with 3¼″ bare wire. [2]
f. Repeat above with 2½″ bare wire. [2]

Assembly:

a. Hold the 8 flowers together with the bottoms even. Pull 2 down to set under the top 2. Pull 4 down to set just under these.
b. Use pliers to spiral the bottom 1″ firmly.
c. Hold 1 of each size fern together. Spiral the bottom 1″. Repeat with remainder.
d. Add 1 on each side of the flower spiral.
e. Grip the taller of the florets plus 2 tall ferns on the back side of the spray, and bend away from the remainder of the sections.
f. Use a 10″ piece of bare wire. Allow a small piece to hang free and bind on the back side of the pin to the taller sections. Use the "jewel" method and keep the windings close and even. Twist the end to the first free end. Trim and press into the pin.
h. Arc the ferns around the back of the flowers to point out on each side.
i. Use pliers to curl the bottom of the stem.

RING, BIRTHSTONE, DOMED

Materials

#25 gold wire
8 inches of beads, the color of your birthstone

Dome petal
Basic 5
Rows 10

Procedure:

a. Fold the first 12″ of bare wire and fold in half again.
b. Twist to the feed wire 3 times. Set the loops on top of one another.

c. Push over the basic 5 beads. Repeat the fold of wire with 6″ of bare wire closely against the 5 beads.
d. Complete the petal.

e. Make the final twist very tightly against the petal and cut free, leaving ¼″ bare wire. Press this into the back of the petal.

f. Cut the long loops at the center point.
g. Work a 4-strand braid as described in "Bracelet, Four-Strand Braid." This is the shank of the ring.
h. Braid until the shank fits around the finger, to meet the petal on the opposite side.
i. Cut the short loops open at the center point.
j. Twist 1 wire of the braid to 1 wire of the short loop end very tightly against the petal.
k. Cut and trim to within ⅛″ and press into the back side of the dome.
l. Repeat with the remaining 3 ends of wire.
m. Use pliers to press the ends firmly into the back of the petal.

RING, CLUSTER

Materials

#28 gold wire
Assorted colors of single beads

Procedure:

a. Cut 9 5½″ pieces of wire.
b. Pick up 1 bead on one wire.
c. Fold ½″ of wire over the bead and spiral firmly down.
d. Repeat this with another color bead on the opposite end of the wire.

e. Repeat with each of the remaining wires.
f. Allow the ½″ to be free and spiral the remaining straight wire of 3 together.
g. Repeat for 2 more units.
h. Allow the ½″ to be free and braid the 3 units together closely and firmly.
i. Shape this over the finger by twisting just under the ½″ spirals.
j. Fan out the cluster.

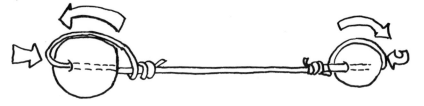

RING, DAISY

Materials

#25 gold wire
Any color desired for daisy
White petals for the center

Daisy:

Allow 4″ of bare wire and make 6–1″ loops, all on one wire. Cut free, leaving 4″ bare wire.

Center:

Allow 4″ of bare wire and make a 10-bead 3-row crossover as described in the daisy necklace instructions. Cut free, leaving 4″ of bare wire.

Assembly:

a. Set the center over the daisy and draw all wires to one side of the unit.

b. Make a 4-strand braid as described in "Bracelet, Four-Strand Braid" to fit the finger.

c. Slip 1 end wire through the starting underside wire, then twist with all other ends.

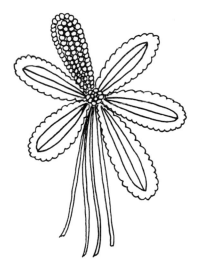

d. Trim close to ring and press back into the underside of the daisy.

RING, INDIAN BEAD

Materials

#32 gold wire
White and a few of any color bead

Procedure:

a. Cut 15″ of wire free from spool.

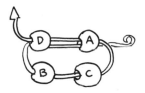

b. String 4 white beads and draw wire, as indicated, 3″ from one end.

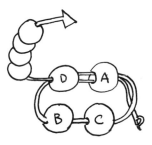

c. String 6 white on the long end. String from right to left. Draw through A bead only.

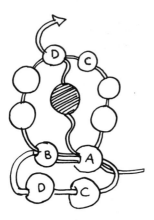

g. Add a colored bead, draw through D position, draw tight.

h. Repeat e, f, and g for a proper fit around the finger, usually 10 circles.

i. To end, string the last D position through the first C and D positions. Go back 1 row and draw through another bead. Trim ends. String the first A position through the last C and D positions. Go back 1 row and draw through another bead. Trim.

d. Add 1 colored bead and draw through D bead. Now draw tight.

e. String 2 white and draw through C and B, tight.

f. String 6 white, draw through A position, but not tight.

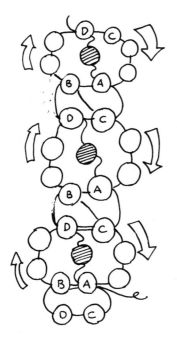

11

Holiday
Workshop

The ornaments and decorations in this chapter will add a glow of warmth to the holiday season. You will enjoy making them, and they are sure to become lasting treasures.

We suggest trying some of the following variations for added enrichment.

Make the Christmas wreath in white crystal and add gold beaded fruit to the center.

Use the wreath to hold a bowl of nuts.

Several Christmas roses can be placed across the center of a buffet table.

Adorn gift packages with mistletoe or poinsettia or snowflakes.

The Chanukah menorah can be made in different colors and presented to each child in the family.

Add to your collection gradually and use them year after year.

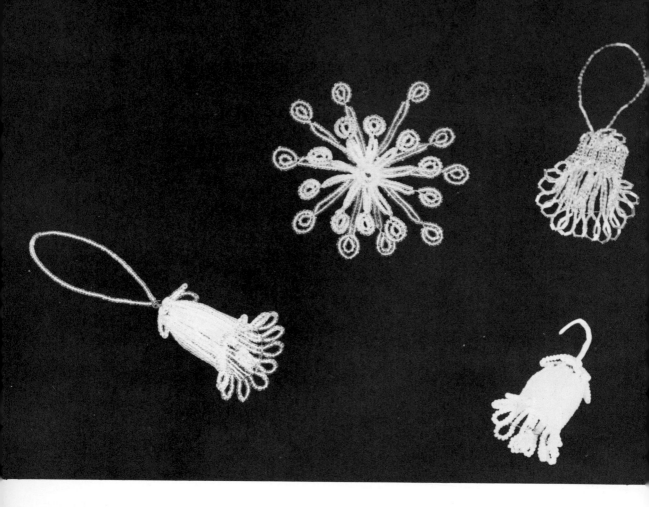

BELLS

ANNIVERSARY BELLS

Pattern used for Christmas ornament

Materials

#26 silver or #25 gold wire
Silver, gold, or white pearl (depending upon the occasion)
#34 lacing wire in matching color
Yellow or white tape

Bell:	13—3″ loops, all on one wire. Keep loops close at base.
Clapper:	½″ 4-row crossover. 2 hanging wires beaded for 1¼″.
Top:	6—¾″ loops, all on one wire. Oval in shape.

Make in pairs and join together with ribbon to form a bow.

CHRISTMAS BELLS I

Materials

#26 silver or #25 gold wire
Silver or gold beads
#34 lacing wire to match

Bell: 22–4″ loops, all on one wire. Keep loops close at base.

Clapper: ½″ 4-row crossover. 2 hanging wires beaded for 1⅝″.

Top: 6–1″ loops, all on one wire. Oval in shape.

The hanging wires of the Christmas bells may be formed into a hook and hung on the branches of the Christmas tree. Or a 6″ loop of beads may be added to the bell as a hanger.

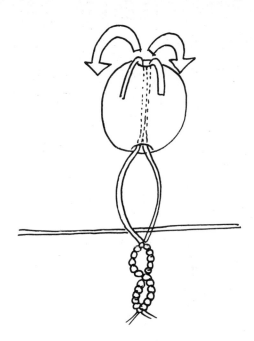

CHRISTMAS BELLS II

Materials

#26 silver or #25 gold wire
Gold or silver beads
One strand of any color crystal
#34 lacing wire to match
A single large bead for the clapper (size of a tree garland)

Clapper:

a. Cut a 2″ piece of bare wire.
b. Fold in half and make a tiny loop in the center.
c. Twist four times.
d. String this wire through the single large bead.
e. Press the 2 end wires across the bottom of the bead to lock it tightly to the loop. (The loop becomes the hanger.)
f. String the hanger on the feed wire, to float freely over the beads.
g. Measure 3″ of beads. With the large bead inside, make a loop.

h. Turn the loop with the oval side down. Allow the clapper to hang at the bottom and spiral the loop.

Bell:

a. Continue on the same wire and make 12–2¼″ loops, all on one wire. *Do not cut free.*
b. Lace across the 12 loops ½″ down.
c. Set the clapper to the inside and close the bell with 3 twists of the end wires.

Base:

a. Continue on the same wire and make: 6–1¼″ loops to fit around the base of the bell.
b. Cut away from spool and twist ends.

Shaping:

Shape the base of the bell like a cup. Press the tips of all loops outward.
Press the base loops up, around the bell.
Twist the end wires of the lacing and set to the inside.
Cut excess wire.

SINGLE BELLS

Materials

#26 silver or #25 gold wire

Any color beads to harmonize with package trim

#34 lacing wire to match working wire

Bell: 10—2½″ loops, all on one wire. Like other bells.

Clapper: ½″ 4-row crossover. 2 hanging stems beaded for 1″.

Top: 5—¾″ loops, all on one wire.

Coil ends around a pencil and attach to gifts for decoration. All bells are assembled the same way.

Assembly:

a. Narrow all loops of the bell.

b. Lace each bell ⅓ of the way down from the top.

c. Form into a circle with finer part of the lacing facing out.

d. Join the lacing wire and twist for ½″.

e. Cut away all but ¼″. Tuck to inside of bell.

f. Twist the hanging wires of the bell together once.

g. Bring one end around to the opposite side of the circle by weaving it in and out around the base of the loops.

h. Join the 2 wires together and twist twice. Stand them upright.

i. Insert the clapper into the bell.

j. Twist clapper wires and bell wires together twice.

k. Form "top" into a circle and place snugly against top of bell.

l. Twist all wires together 3 or 4 times and wrap with tape.

m. Wind ribbon around tape and secure at the ends with glue.

SNOWFLAKE

Materials   3 STRANDS

#28 silver wire

Clear crystal or white irridescent beads

White tape

Row 1: ¾″ beaded stem, 6-bead loop wrapped once, ¾″ beaded stem. Twist the 2 stems together. Make 10 units, all on one wire.

Row 2: 1″ beaded stem, 8-bead loop wrapped once, 1″ beaded stem. Twist the 2 stems together. Make 10 units, all on one wire.

Center: 1—8-bead loop, wrapped once.

Assembly:

a. Place Row 1 on top of Row 2.

b. Twist all hanging wires twice, just below the beads.

c. Place center on top of both rows and twist all hanging wires once again.

d. Thin out the hanging wires and tape in white.

e. Form hanging wires into a hook to attach to tree; or shorten hanging wires and use as decoration for gift packages.

CANDLE HOLDERS

Materials
#28 silver or #25 gold wire
Any color for flowers with a contrast for centers
Green for leaves
Dark green tape
#18 stem wire

Flowers: 5—9-bead loops wrapped twice, all on one wire
Keep loops very round.

Centers: 9-bead loop wrapped once

Leaves: Basic 6   Pointed top   [2 per
Rows 7   Round bottom flower]

Assembly:
a. Cover a #18 stem wire with tape.
b. Form wire into a spiral around the candle.
c. Form 2 circles at the base of spiral (on same wire).
d. Remove wire from candle. Tape the 2 bottom circles together.
e. Starting at the top, tape on 1 flower and 2 leaves. Space the flowers gracefully around the spiral. Since all candles are a different size, the number of flowers needed will depend upon the candle size. To estimate how many you will need, figure about 1″ between flowers.

CANDLE TRIMMERS

Materials
#28 silver wire for flowers
#26 silver wire for leaves
Any color for flowers with a contrast for centers
Any green for leaves
Green tape
#18 stem wire

9 flowers, 12 leaves per circle.

STYLE I

Flowers: 5—9-bead loops, all on 1 wire   [1]

Centers: 1—3-bead loop   [1]

Leaves: Basic ½″   Semipointed top [12]
Rows 15   Round bottom

STYLE II

Flowers: 5—1″ loops, 3-row crossovers   [1]

Centers: 1—5-bead loop   [1]

Leaves: Basic ½″   Semipointed top [12]
Rows 15   Round bottom

Assembly:

a. Tape a #18 stem wire and form it into a circle. The size of the circle depends upon the size of the candle.
b. Form each flower into a circle and add the centers.
c. Twist all hanging wires three times, just below the flower.
d. Tape hanging wires for 2″.
e. Tape the 9 flowers to the circle, spacing them evenly around; 1½″ of flower stem stands up above the circle.
f. Tape hanging wires of leaves and tape leaves onto circle, spacing them ½″ apart.

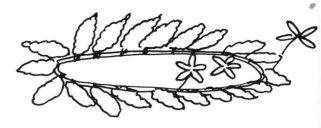

Shaping:
Overlap leaves all the way around the circle. Stand flowers upright with heads facing forward.

200

COASTERS

Materials

#26 silver wire
Any color for flowers (optional)
Green for leaves
Dark green tape
#16 stem wire

Leaves: Basic 1″ Pointed top [11 or 12]
  Rows 11 Round bottom

Flowers may be added between leaves if desired.

Flowers: 1—8-bead loop wrapped twice, 5 all on one wire

Centers: 1—8-bead loop wrapped once

Assembly:

a. Make 2 separate circles with the #16 stem wire to fit loosely around the bottom of a glass. Join them together with tape. (Wires will stand ½″ high.)

b. Place the bottom of a leaf at the base of the circle.

c. Bring hanging leaf wires behind the circle and tape in place.

d. Add one leaf right next to another, all the way around the circle, taping each one to circle individually.

e. After entire circle is completed, all leaves are laced together through the center of the height.

f. If flowers are added, they are set around among the leaves and secured to the circle with tape.

CHANUKAH MENORAH

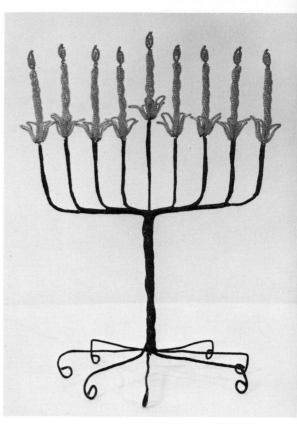

Materials

#25 gold wire
Light orange crystal for main color
Deepest orange crystal for flame color
Yellow tape
#16 and #18 stem wire

String as follows: 14″ of main color, 1″ of flame color, 4″ of main color, 4 beads of flame color.

Procedure: Candle

a.   Hold aside the 4 beads of flame color.
b.   Form the 4″ of main color into a loop.
c.   Hold the loop so the 4 beads slide down on top. Using the 1″ of flame color, make a 3-row petal with the 4 beads as the basic count. Point both ends.
d.   Complete the first loop made into a 4-row crossover.
e.   Turn the candle with the flame facing down.
f.   Fill the space on the feed wire with enough beads to reach the bottom of the crossover loop.
g.   Cut off 3″ of feed wire and feed back through bottom of the loop to anchor.
h.   Spiral the 5 rows of beads like a barber pole.

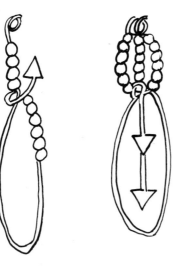

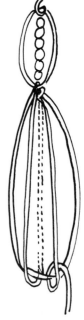

Bottom Holder: 5—1½″ loops, all on one wire

Assembly:

a. Set the candle into the bottom holder and twist all hanging wires together.

b. Have the bottom loops fit all around the base of the candle.

c. Press the loops up with the tips bent out.

Menorah Frame:

a. Tape 1–#16 stem wire. Tape 8 #18 stem wires.

b. Use the #16 wire as the center post of the frame and spiral the #18 wires around this.

c. Tape all horizontal sections together.

d. Tape a candle to the top of each stem. The center candle stands ½″ higher than the rest.

Stems of frame may be dyed with black shoe dye or gilded with "Treasure Gold."

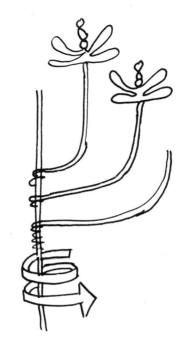

CHRISTMAS LIGHTS

Materials

#28 silver wire
Any color crystal or varied colors for candles
Red for flame
White tape
#16 and #18 stem wire

Follow same procedure as for the Chanukah menorah and make a frame as illustrated. Tape a candle to the top of each stem.

Frame may be finished in "Treasure Gold," which is a wax gilt, or may be painted with black shoe dye to look like wrought iron.

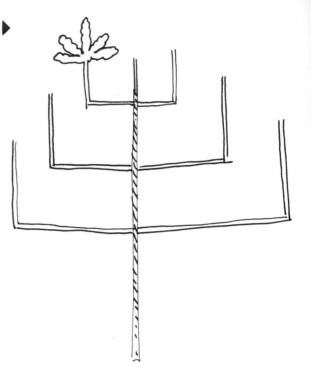

PLACE-CARD HOLDER

Tape 4 candles to a taped 4″ piece of #18 stem wire. Close into a circle.

BIRTHDAY CANDLES

These may be added to a cake individually. Spiral the bare-wire stems all the way down and cover with tape. Roll taped stems tightly into aluminum foil. Insert into cake.

CHRISTMAS ROSE

Materials
#28 gold wire for centers
#26 silver wire for petals and foliage
White crystal for petals
Light or medium green for foliage
Light green tape
Stem beads
#16 stem wire

3 flowers and 4 leaves per branch.

Petals: With white on the wire, add 9 green beads for each petal. Start with a 4″ bottom basic loop. At completion of petal open this loop close to the beads to form a *single* hanging wire.

Basic 9   Pointed top   [5]
Rows 7   Round bottom

After fifth row, cut off 5″ of bare wire and string on light green to complete the petal.

204

Centers: Green. Start with 2″ of bare [6] wire. Make a 5-bead loop. End with 2″ of bare wire. String ½″ of white on each leg. Twist the bare wires of all 6 together to form 1 center.

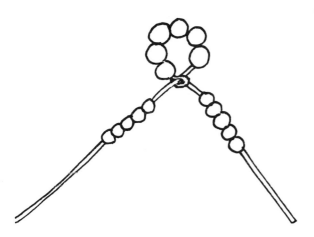

Leaves: Start with 6″ of bare wire. 4—2″ 4-row crossovers, all on one wire. Press the petals flat and cut off 6″ of bare wire. String 3″ of stem beads on to the hanging wires. Tape under beads. Make 4 for 3 flowers.

Assembly of Flower:

a. Hold the 5 petals on top of one another with 3 face up and 2 face down.

b. Twist hanging wires firmly, open petals, and shape like a shallow bowl.

c. Insert the centers. Have 1 straight up and 5 flat around it.

d. Twist all hanging wires once again.

e. Tape stem for 3″.

Assembly of Branch:

a. Tape a 6″ piece of stem wire. Tape a flower to the top with 2″ of stem showing.

b. Add one flower on each side with 2″ of stem showing.

c. Add the leaves ½″ under the flower, all in one spot, evenly around the 3 flowers.

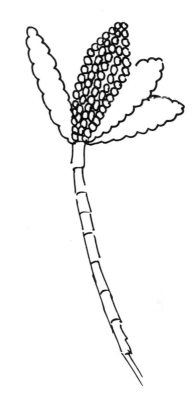

d. Tape down entire stem.

CHRISTMAS TREE

Materials

#26 silver wire
Dark green beads (about 3 double bunches)
Dark green tape
#16 and #20 stem wire
Plaster of Paris
8" flowerpot

Unit 1:   All on one wire. Have 3" of bare
wire at beginning and end.   [5]
    4—1" loops with 3 beads between
loops
    3—¾" loops with three beads between loops
    3—½" loops with no beads between
Repeat the ¾" loops.
Repeat the 1" loops.
Narrow all loops. Fold unit in half
and spiral the entire unit.

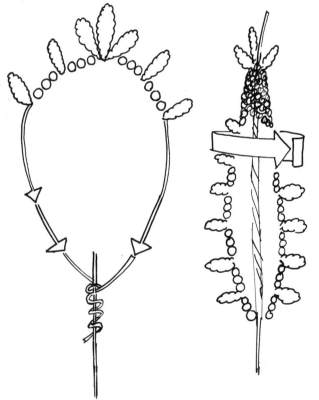

Unit 2:   Same method as Unit 1.   [5]
    5—1" loops with 3 beads between
    4—¾" loops with 3 beads between
    3—½" loops with no beads between
Repeat the ¾" loops.
Repeat the 1" loops.

Unit 3:   Same Method as Unit 1.   [6]
    6—1" loops with 3 beads between
    5—¾" loops with 3 beads between
    3—½" loops with no beads between
Repeat the ¾" loops.
Repeat the 1" loops.

Unit 4: Same method as Unit 1, but do not
spiral. [6]
7–1″ loops with 3 beads between
6–¾″ loops with 3 beads between
3–½″ loops with no beads between
Repeat the ¾″ loops.
Repeat the 1″ loops.

Unit 5: Same as Unit 4. [6]
8–1″ loops with 3 beads between
7–¾″ loops with 3 beads between
3–½″ loops with no beads between

Unit 6: Same as Unit 4. [14]
9–1″ loops with 3 beads between
8–¾″ loops with 3 beads between
3–½″ loops with no beads between
Repeat the ¾″ loops.
Repeat the 1″ loops.

Assembly:

a. Tape 26–8″ pieces of #20 stem wire.
b. Fold one Unit 4 in half. Twist the end
wires, draw the unit taut.

c. Hold this on top of a stem wire with the
tip through the top loop and the remainder
running down the stem. Spiral the entire unit
around the stem.
d. Tape the end wires.
e. Repeat this for all of Units 4 through 6.
f. Tape a #16 stem wire. Tape one of Unit
1 to the top.
g. Add 4 more 1″ under to fit evenly around
the stem.
h. All remaining stems are 1″ under each
other, spaced evenly around.
i. Add Unit 2 to fit evenly around the stem.
j. Continue to add each unit in the same
manner.
k. Unit 4 has ½″ of stem showing.
l. Unit 5 has 1″ of stem showing.
m. 7 stems of Unit 6 make up the next layer;
1½″ of stem shows.
n. The final 7 stems make up the last layer;
2″ of stem shows.

Mix plaster of Paris and set the tree in the
pot.
Fill with plaster for ⅔ of the pot.

CHRISTMAS TREE DECORATIONS

Materials

#26 silver and #32 gold wires
Silver beads, assorted colors of seed beads, as-
sorted colors of bugle beads
A few assorted sequins
A few large beads (8 mm.)

STAR I

a. With silver on the wire, make 5–1¾″
crossover petals, all on one wire.
b. Gently flatten the petal and point the
tips.
c. Twist the 2 end wires together and allow
the hanging wire to remain. This is used to
attach to tree top.
d. Shape as a star.

STAR II

Make a 10-bead circle of bugle beads. Make
the 5 points by using 4 bugles for each point.

STOCKINGS

a. Any color on wire. Work both petals on
one wire.
b. 1″–4-row crossover petal, then a 2″–3-
row crossover petal.
c. End the 3-row petal on top in the following manner: Cut off 3″ of free wire. String
it over the top and up again through the first
loop of this petal. Pull up firmly.
d. Shape as a stocking and use the top
wire to attach to tree.

CANDLES

a. Cut 3″ of #32 gold wire free from spool.
b. Hold one end and string 3 red seed

beads and 3 bugle beads of any color. Center this on the wire.

c. Use one end of the wire and string back into the second red bead and all the bugle beads. *Single beaded stems, Method I. Pull wire down firmly.

d. String a sequin through both wires to the base of the candle.

e. Use the hanging wires to attach to tree branches.

LITTLE PEOPLE

a. Cut 12″ of #32 gold wire free from the spool.

b. Holding one end, string 1 seed bead, 1 sequin, and 1 large bead.

c. Center this on the wire and string back into the sequin and large bead (for the head).

d. Open the wires and put one on each side. Use one wire and string 2 bugle beads and 1 seed bead. Keeping these tightly to the "head," string back through the bugle beads.

e. Repeat this on the opposite side.

f. Now string 2 bugle beads on both wires. Open the wires to put one on each side of the body. Use one wire, and string 3 bugle beads and 1 seed bead. Keeping these tightly against the body, string back into the bugle beads.

g. Repeat this on the opposite side.

h. The two free wires are used to attach to tree.

CANDY CANES

a. String 2″ of white and 2″ of red on silver wire.

b. Separate the two colors and make a 1″ bare-wire loop between them.

c. Push the beads tightly against the loop. Twist bottom end wires and cut free.

d. Spiral the 2 colors together like a barber pole.

e. Make a cane hook at the top.

f. Use the bare-wire loop to hang on to the tree.

GARLANDS

A full string of silver beads may be used to festoon the tree.

BAUBLES

10 bead 4-row crossover petals in assorted colors. Use the end wires to attach to the tree.

CHRISTMAS WREATH

Materials
#26 silver or #26 green wire for leaves
#26 silver wire for all other parts
#32 binding wire
Dark green, medium green, red, black, and yellow crystal
Dark green tape
Large coat hanger

Leaves:	Dark green Basic 1⅜″ Semipointed top [160] Rows 5 Round bottom One 400″ bunch will produce about 50 leaves. Cut all hanging wires to 1¼″ and tape them.
Mistletoe:	Medium green Basic 1″ Round top [16] Rows 5 and bottom Make 2 mistletoe with 3 petals and 1 center.* Make 2 mistletoe with 5 petals and 3 centers.*
CENTERS*:	8 mm. beads in white

Poinsettia

INNER ROW:	Red Basic ¾″ Pointed top [6] Rows 7 Round bottom
OUTER ROW:	Red Basic 1″ As above [9] Rows 9
CENTERS:	6-bead loop in yellow, with the hanging stems beaded in black. Make 6 ranging in length from ¾″ stems to 1¼″ stems. Join all 6 at base of beads.
LEAVES:	Medium green Basic 1½″ Semipointed top [2] Rows 15 and bottom

Assembly:

a. Cover wire hanger with green tape.
b. Make a hook at each end of hanger.
c. Start attaching leaves ¾″ down from hook. Tape on one leaf.
d. Next leaf covers half of the first leaf.
e. Alternate sides going around hanger.
Follow diagram for adding mistletoe and poinsettia.
Close hook before adding poinsettia.
Wire and tape poinsettia to wreath.

Assembly of Mistletoe:

a. Place 3 petals on top of one another face up. Place the other 2 on top of these face down.
b. Twist all hanging wires twice.
c. String centers on their own wire and slide into petals.
d. Tape hanging wire.

Assembly of Poinsettia:

a. Twist hanging wires of centers together and tape.
b. Secure petals of inner row around the hanging wires of centers with #32. Space evenly around.
c. Bind on petals of outer row the same way.
d. Tape all exposed wire and tape down remainder of stem.
e. The two leaves are placed behind the flower and bound on with #32.
f. Secure the entire unit to the wreath with #32.
g. Tape exposed wires.

HOLLY LEAF AND BERRIES

Materials

#26 silver wire for leaves
#25 gold wire for berries
Bright red crystal for berries
Dark green for holly
Dark green tape

Holly: Basic 1¼″   Pointed top
              Rows 11   and bottom

After third row, push down enough beads to fill ⅓ of the row. Make a 4″ bare-wire loop, tightly against the beads. Push down enough beads to fill the next ⅓ of the row. Repeat the bare-wire loop, tightly against the beads. Complete the row. After the basic turn

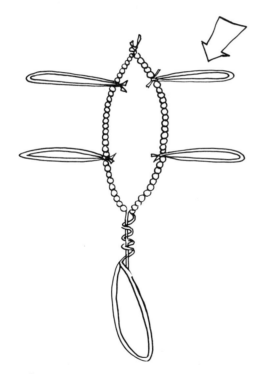

is made, repeat the fourth row to match the loops on the opposite side. All succeeding rows have 6 wires to be used for basic turns. Press down between the side basic wires to arc the sections, while working around. Complete the petal and cut all basic wires as usual.

Berries: Make a 1⅛″ loop. Cut away from spool with 3″ of bare wire. Spiral the loop once to form a small loop on the upper end of the loop. Fold the entire unit in half and draw the end wires through the small loop and down. Spiral the end wires very firmly and use for stem.

Assembly:

a. Tape the bare-wire stems of 2 leaves. Twist the bare-wire stems of 4 berries.
b. Tape all together in a cluster.

MISTLETOE BALL

Materials

#32 wire for jeweling and binding
#26 wire for clusters
Red, green, and a few 8 mm. beads in white
Red tape and green tape
#16 stem wire

Petals: Green
          Basic 1″   Round top   [5]
          Rows 5   and bottom

Centers: 3–8 mm. beads per cluster
Hang 5 clusters from the center of the ball.

Assembly of Mistletoe:

a. String 3–8 mm. beads on to wire.
b. Twist wires a few times to tighten the beads together.
c. Place 3 petals on top of one another face up and 2 face down.
d. Twist hanging wires of all 5 petals together firmly.
e. Fan out with front sides up.
f. Slide in centers and twist all hanging wires tightly, down entire stem. Final stem should measure 2″.
g. Tape down entire stem.

Assembly of Cluster:

a. Holding one mistletoe upward and one downward, tape the hanging stems together.
b. Space the 3 remaining clusters evenly around and bind them tightly with #32 wire.
c. Tape exposed wire.

Assembly of Ball:

a. Tape 3–18″ #16 stem wires with red tape.
b. Form a small hook at the beginning and end of each wire.
c. Jewel entire wire with red beads. End jeweling just short of hooks.
d. Form all wires into a circle by connecting each pair of hooks.

e. Close hooks tightly. Join all circles into a ball shape by sliding one over another.

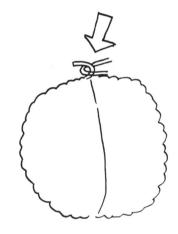

f. Tape exposed hooks.
h. Secure bottom of circle joinings with a small piece of #32. Twist together and cut away excess wire. Cover exposed wire with red tape.
i. Bind mistletoe cluster to the underside of the top joint with #32.
j. Cut away excess wire and tape in red.
k. Hang ball with satin ribbon loop.

PETITE POINSETTIA

Materials

White tape
Flower only, of 3 petite poinsettias, assembled on an 8″ piece of #20 stem wire
3 Christmas Bells II

Assembly of Ring:

a. Bend the top 1″ of the flower stem at right angles.
b. Tape a bell 2″ under the flower.
c. Repeat this for all 3 stems.
d. With 2″ between bell and flower, tape the first stem to the second (between the space of flower and bell).
e. Repeat this with second stem.
f. Close the circle by taping the third stem to the first, in the same manner.
g. Trim excess stem wire.
h. Twist a wire loop around the wreath to hang it.

POINSETTIA RING

Materials

#26 silver wire for petals
#28 gold wire for centers
#32 binding wire
Bright red or white for petals in crystal or chalk
Yellow and light green crystal for centers
Dark green for foliage
Dark green tape
#16 stem wire

Centers: Yellow. Leave 2″ of bare wire at the beginning and end.
3—8-bead loops, all on one wire   [2]
String ½″ of light green on each leg. Twist the hanging wires together.

Petals:

ROW 1: Basic 4   Elongated top   [3]
        Rows 5   and bottom

ROW 2: Basic 4   As above   [7]
        Rows 7

Leaves: Make 2 holly leaves. (See Holly Leaf and Berries.)

Assembly:

a. Tape the top 2″ of a 10″ piece of stem wire.

b. Join the center units together and tape to the top of the stem.

c. Bind on the first row to fit evenly around stem.

d. Tape binding for ½″.

e. Bind on the second row, evenly around stem.

f. Taper and shorten all hanging wires.

g. Tape down entire stem.

h. Tape leaves 2″ under the flower, opposite each other.

Shaping:

Stand all petals straight out.
Form center loops into a circle.
Stand leaves straight out.

SEASON OF BLOOM

SPRING

Andromeda
Apple Blossom
Bleeding Heart
Camellia
Columbine
Daisy: Double-Painted, Field
Dogwood
Flame Violet
Flowering Quince
Gardenia
Globe Phlox
Lily: Calla, Kafir
Lupine
Magnolia, Saucer
Mountain Laurel
Peony
Rhododendron
Scilla
Snowdrop
Stephanotis
Tulip, Parrot
Tulip Tree

SUMMER

Aster: China, Wild
Astilbe
Begonia
Black-Eyed Susan
Blue Lace Flower
Canyon Poppy
Cineraria
Clematis
Coleus
Cupid's-Dart
Cyclamen
Dahlias
Daisy, Shasta
Fabiana
Flowering Crab Apple
Fringed Gentian
Fuchsia
Gaillardia
Gerbera
Gladiolus, Baby
Globe Thistle
Heather
Hibiscus
Indigo
Jasmine
Lily: Atamasco, Red Band
Lythrum
Magnolia, Southern
Marigold, Naughty Marietta
Moss Rose
Mutisia
Ranunculus
Rose Cascade
Salvia
Small Sunflower
Strawflower
Sweet Sultan
Tamarix
Tigerflower
Tree Mallow
Valerian
Veronica
Water Lily
Zinnia

TROPICAL

Anthurium
Bougainvillaea
Chinese Hat Plant
Cup of Gold
Cut-leaf vine
Desert Rose
Night-Blooming Cereus
Orange Blossom
Orchid
Passionflower
Ti Leaves
Wood Rose

FALL

Autumn Leaves
Cattails
Chrysanthemums
Ivy
Pine Cone
Rudbeckia
Scotch Broom
Windflower

INDEX

*Starred flowers are the easiest to make.